_Dr. Brown_

# LEARNING IN OVERDRIVE

Dr. Paul

# LEARNING IN OVERDRIVE

Designing Curriculum, Instruction, and Assessment
from Standards

*A Manual for Teachers*

RUTH MITCHELL, MARILYN CRAWFORD, AND
THE CHICAGO TEACHERS UNION QUEST CENTER

**fulcrum resources**
**Golden, Colorado**

Book design by Deborah Rich
Interior photographs © 1995 Brian David

Library of Congress Cataloging-in-Publication Data

Mitchell, Ruth.
    Learning in overdrive : designing curriculum, instruction, and
assessment from standards : a manual for teachers / Ruth Mitchell,
Marilyn Crawford, and the Chicago Teachers Union Quest Center.
        p.   cm.
        Includes bibliographical references (p.    ) and index.
        ISBN 1-55591-933-2
        1. Curriculum planning—United States—Handbooks, manuals,
etc. 2. Education—United States—Standards—Handbooks,
manuals, etc. 3. Effective teaching—United States—Handbooks,
manuals, etc. I. Willis, Marilyn.  II. Title.
LB2806.15.M48  1995                         95–40972
379.1'54—dc20                             CIP

Printed in the United States of America
0   9   8   7

Fulcrum Publishing
16100 Table Mountain Parkway, Suite 300
Golden, Colorado 80403
(800) 992-2908  •  (303) 277-1623
www.fulcrum-resources.com

# CONTENTS

# Preface

A new spirit is invigorating American education: Teachers are coming out of their isolated classrooms and finding that, working together, they can vastly improve their students' performance and their own professional satisfaction. This manual is intended to help teachers realize the personal and professional benefits of working together on the most important issue in education today—helping students to reach high standards.

Standards—also called outcomes, expectations, and goals—are changing American education from a system driven by inputs and regulations to one judged by results. What should students know and be able to do? How will they know if they know it? And how do we give them all the opportunity to acquire knowledge and abilities? These three questions will focus the educational system for the foreseeable future. So that teachers can take the lead in bringing the standards into their schools and classrooms, we have written this manual to explain how curriculum, instruction, and assessment can be constructed from standards.

What do we mean when we say "standards"? Complete definitions appear in Part Two, Step One, but here we will point to the national standards, listed in Goals 3 and 5 of the eight national education goals. These national goals became law when the Goals 2000: Educate America Act was signed by President Bill Clinton at the end of March 1994. Goals 3 and 5 are listed below.

National standards in all nine of the subjects in Goal 3 and Goal 5 have either been recently developed or are currently in the process of being developed.

Many states have not been waiting for the national standards, however; they have gone ahead and developed their own. Most spectacular of these was Kentucky, where the state educational system was declared unconstitutional and was reconstructed from the ground up in the late 1980s and early 1990s. Kentucky put together six learning goals and then made them practical and functional by developing 75 outcomes.

> **Standards are changing American education from a system driven by inputs and regulations to one judged by results.**

---

### Goals 2000: Educate America Act

3. By the year 2000, American students will leave grades 4, 8, and 12 having demonstrated competency in challenging subject matter including English, mathematics, science, civics and government, economics, foreign languages, arts, history, and geography; and every school in America will ensure that all students learn to use their minds well, so that they may be prepared for responsible citizenship, further learning, and productive employment in our modern economy.

5. By the year 2000, U.S. students will be the first in the world in mathematics and science achievement.

Cities also got into the act: In summer 1993, the Chicago Learning Outcomes Standards Project published the first draft of a wall chart of standards for Chicago public schools.

This manual is intended for use with any set of standards—national, state, or local. It has already been used extensively by teachers in Kentucky and in Chicago, who have added their constructive criticisms to its development. Followed step by step, the manual will take you from a series of abstract statements—the goals, standards, or outcomes—to rich units of instruction. It will help with two other functions: It will give you a tool to separate powerful classroom activities from ones that are merely pleasant, or traditionally used, because you constantly ask, "Is this activity getting my students to the standards?" And the manual promotes professional development of the best kind for teachers—working together on the vital, central issues of teaching and learning.

Stripped down to essentials (because we know teachers don't have a lot of time to read theory), the manual is divided into two major parts (see left).

*Learning in Overdrive* is written in a conversational style so that it gets you into action quickly. It isn't a sacred text that must be followed exactly, and you should feel free to modify it for your own needs. It is the fruit of teachers' experience and is offered to other teachers in the hope of saving them some groping in the dark.

> **Followed step by step, the manual will take you from a series of abstract statements to rich units of instruction.**

---

**Learning in Overdrive**

**Part One:** A summary of a standards-driven unit, so that you can see right away what you're aiming for. This manual is intended to help you produce interdisciplinary units like the one in Part One. The manual can also be use for single disciplines.

**Part Two:** A nine-step process to use in writing your own standards-driven unit, with the full sample unit shown in step nine.

---

## How the Manual Began

*Learning in Overdrive: Designing Curriculum, Instruction, and Assessment from Standards* had its beginnings in a grant program from the Kentucky Department of Education, which in spring 1993 offered teachers an opportunity to design units of study to help students reach Kentucky's standards. At the same time, Calloway County Middle School (CCMS) was a partner in the National Alliance for Restructuring Education (NARE), which was also developing units focused on supporting instruction with the use of microcomputer technology in the classroom. Computers and training were provided to CCMS by Apple Classrooms of Tomorrow, as part of its contribution to NARE. Marilyn Willis, principal at CCMS, with her colleagues Angie Murdock and Rebecca Frizzell—along with several other teachers at the school—seized the opportunity and wrote interdisciplinary units for Kentucky and for NARE.

They soon found that they had to explain the process of designing units to their colleagues, and that meant talking about standards and tasks and where the units fit into the context of a year's instruction. To save repeated explanations, the CCMS group wrote a process manual, the precursor to this one, as a guide.

*Learning in Overdrive* was developed in response to the need to have a process that would help teachers plan instructional units, avoiding the many pitfalls in implementing instruction that is genuinely standards-driven. It is designed for teachers throughout the United States.

## The Process

The process begins with standards and shows teachers how to connect them into interdisciplinary clusters; to devise real-world tasks that will embody the standards; and then how to break the unit into learning segments that will enable students to complete the real-world tasks and attain the standards.

This process begins with the end you want to reach—student performance of a task that embodies selected standards, a process called "backward mapping" because teachers work backward from that task to plan instruction. In this manual as you see it now, after many revisions and rehearsals with different groups of teachers, you will see the process of backward mapping to create instructional units.

This is not the complete picture of backward mapping, as the term is used by its originators, the Coalition of Essential Schools at Brown University in Providence, Rhode Island. For the Coalition, backward mapping includes all aspects of the school. Here we focus only on teachers, giving them tools to design their own tasks culminating in a performance demonstrating mastery of standards and the instruction students need to perform them.

This kind of instruction is called "standards-driven," a phrase you will see frequently in the manual. All the teachers who have tried the process found it hard at first, because standards-driven instruction was totally opposite to the usual way of doing business. This book is intended to help you understand the change and make it your own by developing instruction and assessment for your classroom that is driven totally by standards.

This process is best done as part of a professional conversation with colleagues in a workshop where questions like these will continually arise: What do you want your students to know at the end of the year? What's the best way to ensure that they learn these things? Can all students achieve high standards? How? Can we organize schools, classrooms, and instructional time so students will achieve at high levels?

We urge you to use the manual in a workshop or in collaboration with colleagues, and then keep it as a guide to refer to when designing units to meet standards. It can be used as a stand-alone, but you will miss a great deal if you do not engage in the professional conversation of a workshop.

**What do you want your students to know at the end of the year? What's the best way to ensure that they learn these things?**

## ... And Enjoy!

Please enjoy our manual as you use it. Not the least of the pleasures of designing these standards-driven units is working with colleagues, occasionally arguing, and frequently laughing with them. Working together, teachers can be the powerhouse of new learning, helping students to meet the challenges of the twenty-first century. Working together is guaranteed to be exciting, challenging, and inspiring. It will put a song in your heart and a whistle on your lips.

# ACKNOWLEDGMENTS

This book was completed with assistance from the following people: Rebecca Frizzell, teacher, Calloway County Middle School, Murray, Kentucky; Angie Murdock, teacher, Calloway County Middle School, Murray, Kentucky; Deborah Walsh, director, Chicago Teachers Union Quest Center; Allen Bearden, assistant director, Chicago Teachers Union Quest Center.

With special thanks to: Stacie Carmichael, Kentucky Department of Education; Leslie Salmon-Cox, National Alliance for Restructuring Education; Mary Leer, National Alliance for Restructuring Education; and the teachers of the 1992 Quest Schools, Chicago, Illinois.

Dedicated to the memory of John Kotsakis, former assistant to the president for educational issues, Chicago Teachers Union.

# LEARNING IN OVERDRIVE

# PART ONE

# The End Is the Beginning

*What does a standards-driven unit look like?*

*The opening line of a song from the movie* The Sound of
Music *is, "Let's start at the very beginning, a very good place
to start." Good idea. That makes sense. But what is the beginning? Where do we start? What if we start at the end and work
our way backward, making every choice along the way with the
end in mind? It's just like going on vacation. The first question
is always, "Where do we want to go?" Everything else follows.*

*Learning in Overdrive: Designing Curriculum, Instruction, and Assessment From Standards* is a manual for developing units based on standards, with student achievement measured by performance assessment. Maybe that makes total sense to you. Perhaps it's a foreign language. Regardless of your level of understanding, you all know one thing quite clearly: Education is DIFFERENT, radically and significantly different!

The process is eloquently simple, yet profound. We have struggled with making the concepts clear and the steps "goof-proof," with giving you adequate information to complete the task of writing standards-driven units—giving you information you need to develop expertise without overwhelming you as you begin. In Part One, you will see a standards-driven unit. Then you will move to Part Two, into the nine-step process, with concepts developed in greater detail as you move through each step.

The first thing you need to do is read both parts of the manual all the way through. You need the whole picture before you do anything, and readwhere you are going. And that, as you will soon see, is the key to successful instruction and learning.

> Standards-driven instruction simply means teaching and learning based on students achieving high standards.

## What Is Standards-Driven Instruction?

Standards-driven instruction simply means teaching and learning based on students achieving the high standards discussed in the Preface—a deceptively simple idea. First, set high standards that determine what students need to know and be able to do. Second, do whatever it takes for as long as it takes to teach all students these standards. Third, measure student achievement of these standards by having them perform what they have learned and then comparing that performance to the standards.

Standards-driven instruction moves through these stages in a continuous cycle: Assessment is used to obtain information on student achievement and instruction is adjusted accordingly until all students reach or exceed the standards.

### Reaching High Standards

The single measure of successful instruction is that students are able to perform at high levels according to rigorous standards, even though they may reach that end using a wide variety of methods and time frames.

## What Is a Standards-Driven Unit?

An interdisciplinary standards-driven unit is a chunk of instruction designed to teach standards that fit naturally together. These units are aimed at mastery of a rich task that embodies several standards and requires performance of those standards in order to complete the task. Components of the unit include:

- Standards
- Driving questions that energize instruction
- A culminating task that embodies the standards and answers the driving question
- A description of levels of acceptable performance of the task

- The chunks of instruction and curricular choices used to help students achieve the culminating task, and therefore achieve the standards

These units are interdisciplinary, or cross-disciplinary, or multidisciplinary—any expression you like showing that more than one academic subject is involved. A year's curriculum will consist of several standards-driven units, *although not all instruction occurs in units*. The instruction is rigorous: Students *will* achieve world class standards.

The unit focuses on achievement and performance of rigorous standards rather than on the low-level, hands-on activities that are often a major part of many units of study.

## The Culminating Task and Driving Questions

Each standards-driven unit is energized by *a culminating task*, an engaging real-world activity that embodies all the learner standards and gives students a reason to achieve them. The culminating task includes essential *driving questions* that demand answers, questions that inspire and energize student learning. The culminating task makes up the engine for the standards-driven unit: a meaningful, rigorous task that requires students to achieve and perform the standards selected for the unit.

Not just something that happens at the end of the unit, the culminating task controls everything that happens for the duration of the unit of study. It may involve technology, school-to-work connections, and a wide variety of other teaching strategies ranging from traditional to highly innovative—a full continuum of options. Everything students do in the standards-driven unit is directed toward successful completion of the culminating task, which embodies the standards and answers the driving question. In Steps Four and Five you will find detailed information on culminating tasks and driving questions, and you will learn to build your own tasks.

The standards-driven unit of study is totally focused on achievement of high standards, with all unit activities leading to successful performance of the selected standards on the culminating task.

## How Do You Know Students Achieve Standards?

The key to a successful standards-driven unit is this: When students successfully complete the culminating task, they have successfully achieved every selected standard. Students must actually apply what they have learned and demonstrate mastery of standards. You will learn more about performance assessment in Step Seven, with discussion on portfolios, exhibitions, and rubrics and their construction.

## What Does a Standards-Driven Unit Look Like?

Let's take a look at a sample standards-driven unit. The unit consists of the following parts:

1. The culminating task used to achieve standards
2. The selected standards that students will achieve
3. The teaching sections used in instruction and learning, including the performance assessment rubrics used to measure achievement

What we're showing you is a sample standards-driven unit, a shortened version of the final form. In doing so, we're exemplifying *backward mapping*. You know what you want to achieve, and then you can plan how to get there. Before you look at the unit, let's talk about "just how different is different?" Let's take a look at the kind of teaching, learning, and assessing we're talking about in *Learning in Overdrive*, compared to more traditional units:

|  | Traditional | Learning in Overdrive |
|---|---|---|
| **Time** | 40- to 50-minute periods | Flexible, with sample unit taught up to 4-hour days over 6 to 8 weeks |
|  | Textbook-bound timing based on chapter length | Timed for completing tasks |
|  | Lock step and standardized | Flexible (over varying periods of time) and learner-driven |
| **Instruction** | Textbook-bound teacher-centered | Standards-driven, learner-centered |
|  | Standardized | Individualized |
|  | Breadth over depth | Depth over breadth |
| **Curriculum** | Textbook-driven | Best thinking about what students should know and do |
|  | Fragmented | Interconnected |
|  | Emphasis on basics and coverage | Higher level thinking within and across disciplines |
| **Learning** | *Passive* | *Active* |
|  | Rote | Real world problems |
|  | Predigested information | Learner constructs meaning |
|  | One right answer | Diversity of possibilities |
| **Teaching** | Isolated | Collaborative |
|  | Solitary | Teams |
|  | Bureaucratic | Professional |

This is a summary of some of the differences you may notice as you look at this unit. The best thing to do at this point is to look at a shortened sample unit in order to get a general idea of what a unit might look like.

**The Sample Unit**

"This Land Is Your Land, This Land Is My Land!" is an interdisciplinary unit designed for a secondary school. Think about it as a model you can adapt to your own circumstances, schedule, and resources. "This Land Is Your Land, This Land Is My Land" is team taught, and involves math, language arts, science, social studies, art, and technology teachers.

First you will see the culminating task in its final form. Next, you will see a one-page summary of the standards and major components driving the unit, followed by a one-page graphic that gives you an overview of all the learning segments—the chunks of instruction and learning that compose the unit.

Remember, this unit is an *example*, with several disciplines included so you can see how this type of instruction can work. Other units might look quite different. Your unit does not have to include as many disciplines, as many standards, or take as much time as this one does. You might choose to write a much simpler unit. That's perfectly fine!

As you look at the sample, pay closest attention to the structure: how the standards and the culminating task are matched, how the learning sections work together so students complete the culminating task and achieve the standards.

The unit is shown in fully developed format in Step Nine. Take a look. Let's see where we are going.

## THIS LAND IS YOUR LAND, THIS LAND IS MY LAND!

**An Overview**

1. The Culminating Task

2. The Standards for the Unit

3. Unit Broken Into Learning Sections

4. Overview of Six Learning Sections

# THE CULMINATING TASK

*Students will plan, organize, and carry out for the community a Pure Water Day. The day's activities will focus on issues of water purity in the community. These activities will be designed to answer the driving question: Is the quality of our community's water affected by individual uses of land?*

As private citizens, we use a wide variety of chemicals in and around our homes, chemicals that have the potential to pollute the earth's water supplies. We use lawn fertilizer, pesticides, household chemicals, paint, thinner, motor oil, antifreeze, and many other common chemicals. We make frequent choices about how to use these chemicals, and we make choices about how to dispose of old or excess chemicals when we no longer need them. As individuals, our choices seem insignificant. Collectively, however, we may have a major impact—either positive or negative—on the community's water supply.

Your community is struggling with finding a balance between protecting personal freedom and protecting the water supply for the good of the entire community. How can a community protect its water supply from contamination by common chemicals (such as pesticides, fertilizer, paint, paint thinner, motor oil) while maintaining individual citizens' rights to choose how they will use these chemicals in and around their homes and farms?

Your school has been asked to plan and implement Pure Water Day in order to present information and propose action about water purity in the community. As a result of your research and your proposals, you may persuade the community that water purity is in danger and regulations should be contemplated; or that the common water source is safe and no action is necessary; or that action may be needed in the future if present trends continue.

On Pure Water Day, you will design and present an informational exhibit for the public, including:

1. Models to show how water can become polluted by human activity through the water cycle.
2. An analysis of your community's opinions and practices in relation to pure water supply and use of chemicals, including charts and graphs to interpret data.
3. The results of scientific inquiry testing your hypothesis on proposed projects that will impact social attitudes and practices, based on information gathered in the public opinion poll.
4. A collection of editorials, published in newspaper format, presenting student opinions on the role of law and the U.S. Constitution in balancing personal freedom vs. community welfare, specifically related to water issues.
5. A presentation of your conclusions and your recommendations to the community for action. The project might be focused on ensuring the purity of water now or in the future, such as setting up collection points for discarded chemicals, paint, and motor oil; researching alternatives to chemical pesticides and fertilizers; or writing a children's book on the sources of water. Or your project might be focused on informing the public that there is not a problem. You should make your decision based on all the information you have collected.

## The Standards for the Unit

### "This Land Is Your Land, This Land Is My Land!"

| Language Arts | Social Studies | Math |
|---|---|---|
| Read wide variety of materials, including technical information | Understand democratic principles of justice, equality, responsibility, and freedom and apply to real-life problems | Understand and accurately use statistics, including collecting and organizing data, then using it as a powerful tool for decision making |
| Speak and write to communicate information and ideas to various audiences for various purposes | Understand U.S. Constitution and its relationship to law, individual freedom, and society | |

| Science | Workplace Skills | The Arts |
|---|---|---|
| Know and understand scientific methods and use them to solve real-life, everyday problems | Organize and plan for a purpose | Use knowledge of the principles of design to communicate ideas clearly |
| Complete tasks and create products that identify systems and components and the ways the parts work together | Find and use information to meet specific demands, explore interests, or solve problems | |
| Understand water cycle and interaction between water cycle and pollutants on earth's surface | Use computers and other technology to collect, organize, and communicate information and ideas | |

## Unit Broken Into Learning Sections

---

**Pure Water Day: A Community Exhibition**
(Math/Science/Language Arts/Social Studies/Art/Technology)

Present informational exhibition for the public, including models of water cycle, analysis of public opinion and practices, and results of scientific inquiry exploring proposed projects that will impact social attitudes and practices, and proposals for action that will inform the community that there is not a problem or that will prevent or correct a problem now or in the future.

---

↑ ↑

**Learning Section 5**
(All teachers)
Plan for implementation of Pure Water Day.

**Learning Section 6**
(All teachers)
Prepare for project based on information you have collected and present on Pure Water Day.

↑ ↑

**Learning Section 3**
Inquiry
(Math/science)
Use scientific inquiry to form and test hypothesis on proposal for projects that will impact social attitudes and practices identified in public opinion poll.

**Learning Section 4**
Scientific Student Editorials
(Language Arts/Social Studies)
Present opinions on the role of law and the U.S. Constitution in balancing personal freedom vs. community welfare, specifically related to water issues.

↑ ↑

**Learning Section 1**
Public Opinion Poll
(Math/language arts/social studies/technology)
Develop poll to measure public opinion, knowledge, and practices. Collect and interpret data, presenting conclusions with charts and graphs.

**Learning Section 2**
Water Cycle Models
(Science/Art)
Learn about water cycle and how it gets polluted using models.

## Overview of the Six Learning Sections

### *Learning Section One: Public Opinion Poll*

In Learning Section One students develop an instrument and process for measuring public opinion and practice concerning the local community's understanding of the issues regarding individual use of chemicals and the purity of water supply. What does the community know, what does it think, and what does it actually do? Students research current trends and issues on water quality and use this information as a basis for developing a poll to measure public opinion, knowledge, and practices. They learn to construct good questions, to use population sampling, to collect data in different ways—then they collect their data. They analyze and interpret the data with the support of technology, then develop conclusions and explain them using charts and graphs to summarize their data and support their conclusions. They present their work so the public can understand clearly what they find.

### *Learning Section Two: The Water Cycle*

How does the water cycle work? In Learning Section Two students will design a model explaining how water is produced and how it gets polluted. Students research the water cycle, focusing on developing thorough understanding of the water cycle and how water can become polluted by human activity on the earth's surface. Students learn to identify and quantify potential pollutants, including chemical toxicity. They develop a model for conveying understanding of the water cycle and possible sources of pollution from household and yard chemicals. The model must communicate clearly and accurately how the water cycle works, and exactly how water can be polluted by the use and disposal of chemicals on the earth's surface.

### *Learning Section Three: Scientific Inquiry*

In Learning Section Three students use scientific inquiry to test their hypothesis about which practices, if any, need to be changed if we are to ensure pure water or about what information is lacking or needs to be corrected. Students learn the scientific inquiry cycle then use conclusions from the public opinion poll and knowledge from their research to identify potentially harmful practices, areas of misinformation or lack of information. They use this information to formulate a hypothesis about practices or information that need changing, then test that hypothesis using scientific inquiry. They use their conclusions to plan an action proposal for Pure Water Day.

### *Learning Section Four: Persuasive Editorial*

What is the appropriate balance between individual rights and community good in relation to our local water supply? In Learning Section Four students study the U.S. Constitution and Bill of Rights, focusing on the rights of the individual vs. community rights and responsibilities. After observing a debate sponsored by the local bar association, participating in seminars in addition to a wide variety of other activities, students study editorial writing and then write their personal opinion based on a study of the U.S. Constitution and law, their research in Learning Section One, and their understanding of the water cycle and pollution in Learning Section Two. Finally, they compile their editorials for dissemination throughout the community using newspaper format.

### Learning Section Five: Planning Pure Water Day

In Learning Section Five students develop and implement a plan for putting on Pure Water Day for the community, focusing on public awareness of the event and a high level of public participation. Students use workplace skills to organize and prepare for Pure Water Day. They learn to work together, using organization and leadership to get the job done. They focus on publicity and engaging the public, writing letters and news articles to make the community aware of Pure Water Day.

### Learning Section Six: Prepare Presentation of Final Proposal

In Learning Section Six students prepare a presentation of their final proposal, to be made to a community panel in a public forum on Pure Water Day. The proposal should be based on understanding of the water cycle and possible pollution, research on community practices and opinions, the results of scientific inquiry, and personal position on the rights of the individual citizen in relation to the good of the community in relation to the water supply. Students present their proposal to a scoring committee on Pure Water Day, with the public welcome to attend.

### Pure Water Day

Finally, students present Pure Water Day to the community, including a public exhibition of their scientific experiments, their water cycle models, the analysis of community opinions and practices, and their collected editorials in addition to presenting project proposals publicly throughout the day. All the learning sections move students toward Pure Water Day.

# ARE YOU READY?

*Now you know what a unit looks like and you know what we're aiming for. We've also thrown a lot of new terms at you, such as standards and culminating tasks. Don't worry—all will be explained in Part Two. Turn the page and begin a step-by-step journey to learning in overdrive.*

# PART TWO

# Nine Steps to Standards

# Selecting Standards

*Do you remember how it was? Sixteen years old and you're going to take the driver's license exam. Everyone, friends and foe alike, knows where you're going. They only give the test once a week, during second and third period classes on Tuesdays. A dead giveaway.*

*You are thrilled. And totally ill. You have to drive just so, with a state trooper in uniform sitting in the front seat beside you. You even have to parallel park with that trooper sitting beside you! It seems impossible.*

*But what if you pass? And what if you don't pass? Everyone will know. It will be so embarrassing. What if you can't perform what the state says you have to be able to do in order to drive? If you want to drive, you have to meet the standard. The one standard.*

*Now it is fourth period, and you are flashing your new license around instead of concentrating on English. Sixteen years old and free at last! Those standards are a fine thing. A mighty fine thing.*

**What You Will Learn in Step One**

1.  Learn more about standards. Take a closer look at what standards really are by looking at the three types of standards: content, performance, and opportunity-to-learn.

2.  Look at examples of standards from a variety of sources (with additional information available in Appendix A).

3.  Learn the difference between standards and activities. Initially it can be very difficult to distinguish between content standards, what you want students to know, and the activities that students participate in to learn and demonstrate that they have learned. Learn the critical difference.

4.  Collect copies of standards for all subjects you might possibly include in your unit.

5.  Select standards you will address for a full year's instruction for all subjects, or select several standards from each discipline for a single unit.

6.  Don't bite off more than you can chew by selecting too many standards.

*One of the most important questions a teacher can ask is, "What do you want students to know and be able to do?" In Step One, that's what you are going to do—decide what you want your students to know and be able to do.*

## Learn More About Standards

There are three types of standards you should know about: content standards, performance standards, and opportunity-to-learn standards. In this manual we are primarily concerned with content standards, but you should know enough to be able to follow some of the discussions about the other two kinds. Here are definitions:

- Content standards are fixed goals for learning. They lay out what students should know and be able to do—the knowledge and skills essential to a discipline that students are expected to learn. Student performance is measured according to these fixed standards, as opposed to comparing students to one another. Students all over the world can be measured against the same standards. "All students can learn at high levels" means that all students can attain proficiency on rigorous "world class" standards, standards benchmarked to the highest that exist anywhere in the world—given time, support, and instruction that meets their needs. The result is fixed; the instruction varies. Those fixed goals are called content standards.

- Performance standards tell you what a student product should look like if it meets the standards. They describe levels of performance and acceptable kinds of evidence that the content standards have been met. Some people say that content standards show you the rail and performance standards tell you how high you have to jump. Setting performance standards requires looking at student work, using a process of moving back and forth between content standards and student work, adjusting the standard (probably upward) in view of the student response, and rejudging the student work in light of the standard. Developing performance standards in this way, with a group of teachers, administrators, parents, and students, is one of the single most valuable activities that could be devised for the improvement of teaching and learning.

- Opportunity-to-learn (OTL) or delivery standards are descriptions of the conditions necessary for students to achieve the content standards, such as physical facility, access to materials, resources available, and skilled teachers. They are the subject of debate and controversy, because they could be construed as a way back into inputs and regulations, the kind of education we thought we were changing. In a way, this manual is part of opportunity-to-learn standards: It is giving you the means of providing opportunities to your students to meet the standards.

Now you know something about standards. Just hang on to the idea that this manual deals with content standards, and when we refer to the term "standard(s)" from here on, we will automatically be referring to "content standards" only.

You may be confused because you're thinking, "My state doesn't have standards, we have outcomes." Some may have goals or core curricula or academic expectations or learner outcomes. Basically, all these are versions of the same thing: They are statements of what students are expected to know and be able to do.

Even where states have general statements of expected behaviors, such as "communicating well," or "being a responsible citizen," they usually also have curriculum frameworks or statements about expected knowledge and skills in roughly disciplinary divisions. These are usually the basis of curriculum and assessments.

You may choose to use the national standards, such as the National Council on Teachers of Mathematics (NCTM) Standards. You will get more information on these national standards a bit later in Step One.

Regardless of your source, looking closely at standards will focus your attention tightly on exactly what you want your students to know and be able to do. And that's a good thing!

> **Some states may have goals or core curricula or academic expectations or learner outcomes. Basically, all these are versions of the same thing: They are statements of what students are expected to know and be able to do.**

### Look at Examples of Standards

So what do standards look like? Here's an example from one set of standards you've probably already heard of, the National Council of Teachers of Mathematics (NCTM) Curriculum and Evaluation Standards for School Mathematics (Reston, Virginia: NCTM, 1989, p. 105).

---

**Sample Math Standard from NCTM**

In grades 5 through 8, the mathematics curriculum should include exploration of statistics in real-world situations so that the students can:

- systematically collect, organize, and describe data;

- construct, read, and interpret tables, charts, and graphs;

- make inferences and convincing arguments that are based on data analysis;

- evaluate arguments based on data analysis;

- develop an appreciation for statistical methods as powerful means for decision making.

---

Please note some important features of this mathematics standard. The standard does not dictate curriculum content: "Exploration of statistics in real-world situations" leaves plenty of room for creative choice of material. Further, the standard tells you what someone who understand statistics at a middle-school level should be able to do in general terms, but gives you enough specifics to be able to judge whether your classroom activities are in line with the standard. Finally, the verbs describe assessible actions, since standards or outcomes must be assessable. Otherwise, how would we know when students met them?

> **The standard does not dictate curriculum content.**

To give you some idea of what various kinds of content standards look like, here's a selection. These are chosen just to give you the form and wording of a standard, so you will begin to understand more clearly what we are talking about. They are not divided by grade or age. You can get complete information standards from the sources listed in Appendix A.

## Mathematics

- Gather information and communicate ideas by measuring.

- Communicate ideas by quantifying with whole, rational, real, and/ or complex numbers.

- Demonstrate understanding of data concepts related to both certain and uncertain events.

- Organize and communicate ideas by algebraic and geometric reasoning.

- Organize information and communicate ideas by visualizing space configurations and movements.

## Language Arts

- Construct meaning from a variety of print materials for a variety of purposes through reading.

- Communicate ideas and information to a variety of audiences for a variety of purposes through writing and speaking.

- Use research tools to locate sources of information and ideas relevant to a specific need or problem.

- Understand grammar and mechanics, and why and when they are important to successful communication.

## Science

- Use scientific skills to solve specific problems in real-life situations.

- Identify and describe systems, subsystems, and components and their interactions.

- Identify, compare, and contrast patterns to understand and interpret past and present events and predict future events.

- Use models and scales to explain or predict the organization, function and behavior of objects, materials, and living things.

- Understand the tendency of nature to remain constant or move toward a steady state in closed systems.

- Understand the changing earth with reference to surface and subsurface activity, the earth's composition, and its geological history.

- Understand the structure of the universe and the forces affecting it.

### Social Studies

- Demonstrate understanding of continuity and change in historical events, conditions, trends, and issues.

- Apply democratic principles such as justice, equality, responsibility, and choice to real-life situations.

- Explain issues of importance to citizens in a democracy, including authority, power, civic action, and rights and responsibilities.

- Demonstrate an understanding of the structure of the U.S. government and the role of the Constitution.

- Demonstrate knowledge of the major events of U.S. history.

- Demonstrate an understanding of the geographic interaction between people and their surroundings.

- Recognize varying social groupings and institutions and know their beliefs, customs, norms, and roles.

- Make economic decisions regarding production and consumption of goods and services related to real-life situations.

- Construct meaning from and/or communicate ideas and emotions through movement, sound, and artifacts in two or three dimensions.

- Analyze own and others' artistic products and performances according to aesthetic criteria.

These examples give you some idea of what standards look like in the academic disciplines. Put them in your own language, if you like. The point is to understand clearly what all those activities you love to do with your students must be moving them toward if the activities are to be effective. That's what standards-driven instruction is—instruction pushing students to the kinds of knowledge and abilities we've listed here.

**To decide what standards you should use, the first step is to find out whether your state or school district has adopted standards.**

To decide what standards you should use, the first step is to find out whether your state or school district has adopted standards. Then you can get a copy, discuss them with colleagues so that you understand them and are able to use them. If your district or state has not adopted standards or outcomes, you could use the national standards. National standards have been published for mathematics, arts education, geography, U.S. history, social studies, and science (Benchmarks for Science Literacy). Sources for obtaining copies of these standards, or drafts of emerging standards, are listed in Appendix A.

## Learn the Difference Between Standards and Activities

Warning: Activities are NOT standards! The deepest, darkest, biggest, baddest monster in standards-driven learning is to let teaching activities drive instruction rather than having content standards determine instruction and curriculum. One of the most important thing you will do in writing your unit of study is to learn the difference between content standards and teaching activities.

When teachers begin working on standards-driven instruction, they sometimes find it hard to distinguish a standard from an activity or an objective. They either think in terms of activities ("Well, I can get my students to build their dream houses") or in small "objectives" such as the use of capital letters and punctuation. Learning to identify what standards look like in academic subjects is critical to successful standards-driven instruction. Activities and objectives are not standards.

One way to get at standards is to think of the five or six "big ideas" that you want students to learn from your class or your course—the ideas that are so important that students must know them or they really won't know anything about the subject.

Big ideas are, for example, evolution in biology; understanding patterns in mathematics; the ability to write for some purpose to a specific reader in language arts; how we understand history, always from the historian's point of view; and so on. Try writing down the critical things (it might only be one, but it shouldn't be more than five or six) that you know are the center of what you teach.

Standards are the enduring things your students will know and be able to do. Activities are what they (and, hopefully to a lesser extent, you) do to attain those enduring standards. For example:

Standard:   Students demonstrate understanding of data concepts related to measures of central tendency.

Activity:   Students survey peers for attitudes on tobacco use and analyze the data collected, including mean, median, and mode.

The survey is the means to an end—it's an activity. The end—the standard—is the ability to understand, manipulate, and interpret the data. There is a critical difference. Standards must be based on what students need to know and be able to do. Standards first; activities follow.

In Step One you are concerned only with standards. At this point, you should NOT think how you will help students reach those standards or what the topic of your standards-driven unit will be. If you have already decided that

> **Activities and objectives are not standards.**

at this point, you're in trouble. Look where students are going, not how you are going to help them get there. Don't think about teaching activities, the topic of your unit, or lesson plans. Just think content standards.

## Collect Copies of Standards

**You can collect standards from a variety of sources.**

To start working on your unit, you will need to have before you the standards that make sense for your state, district, or school. If you already have standards you are required to follow, this step will be easy—just go get copies of your materials that have the standards listed. If not, you have a choice: You can collect standards from a variety of sources. Even if you already have state, district, or school standards, many of these materials can still be of great help in clarifying your local standards. It's worth taking a look!

While we don't recommend it, if you are using textbooks to organize instruction and you have no other standards available, you can use the unit and chapter headings to write a list of "what you want your students to know and be able to do." This only works to the extent that your textbook actually mirrors what you want your students to know and be able to do, and many textbooks (especially in mathematics) lag behind the national standards. So proceed with caution!

## Select Standards

The best units of study begin with the big picture, with the year's instruction in a wide variety of disciplines. They start with a bird's-eye view of the year, getting more and more tightly focused every step of the way—starting with binoculars, ending with a microscope! In Step One, you have one task and one task only: to select an array of standards that will be addressed during the year.

**The best units of study begin with the year's instruction in a wide variety of disciplines.**

Your choice will be to select standards for the entire year (or other large block of time) for every subject you will teach OR to select a smaller number of standards from several subjects. You will select standards for your unit from the list you compile, so selecting standards for the year in all subjects is the most sophisticated way to develop a unit. But it is also the most overwhelming!

Once you get the hang of this process, that may be what you choose to do. If you are a beginner, however, it is probably easier to select several standards you know you want to address in several different subjects, standards that might possibly be included in a unit.

At any rate, you need to select standards for all subjects or curriculum areas you will possibly be including in any of your units of study.

## Don't Bite Off More Than You Can Chew

One more bit of advice and you can get to work. Don't bite off more than your kids can chew! Attaining standards takes time, and we educators are programmed to "cover the book" rather than to take time to "go deep" and let content standards determine the pace of instruction.

If you select too many learner standards, will your students have enough time to learn? Will they know and be able to perform tasks related to those standards? Less is more, fewer is better. Keep it simple!

## Your Turn! Step One

*Instructions: List the learner standards for each separate subject you might possibly include in your unit. CAUTION: THIS SOUNDS SIMPLE. IT'S NOT!*

1.  You will need a package of 4 x 6 index cards and a way to color code different subjects (such as colored marker pens). A highlighter pen can also be useful.

2.  You will need copies of standards such as the NCTM Standards, state, district, or national standards or outcomes, textbooks, and any other materials that determine what students in your school are required to learn.

3.  List the learner standards for each subject or curriculum area that might possibly be included in your study—either for the year or for less than a year.

4.  Record every single standard on a separate card, using different colors for each subject or curriculum area. Be as concise as you can, making sure each standard is clearly stated and is fully understandable.

5.  Option: Highlight key words in standards if you choose, particularly if they are long statements.

6.  Don't lose the cards!

---

### REMINDERS

*   Decide what your students will know and be able to do for each subject for the year or part of the year (use your textbook unit headings only if all else fails).

*   Keep your focus on standards now. Activities will follow.

*   Select only the standards for which you have time.

# What's in a Standard?

*There was a parakeet named Charlie—a member of a young family of humans with three rambunctious kids—who learned to talk. He learned all the regular parakeet words about being a pretty bird and about crackers. But he also learned to say something from the sometimes overwhelmed mother of this young, energetic family. When things got exciting around the house, Charlie would scream at the top of his parakeet lungs, "I told you and told you and told you!"*

*P.S. Charlie died the day Mom brought the fourth child home from the hospital. August 13, 1968. True story.*

## What You Will Learn in Step Two

1.  Understand the need to include clear components. Review the need to include clear components in all standards.

2.  Clarify standards. Decide which standards are complete, which need expansion, and which need simplification. Then do it!

3.  Identify standards that are complete. Identify standards that have a broad main heading with more specific components listed, similar to an outline.

4.  Identify standards that need more detail. Identify and expand standards that have a broad main heading but do not have specific components that clearly outline what the broad standard means.

5.  Identify standards that need to be simplified. Identify and simplify standards that are broken into specific, highly detailed components and need to be simplified for this process.

*Once you have selected standards—either for the entire year or for part of the year—you are ready to take the next step in developing your unit: looking more closely at what is included in those standards. Look closely at the standards you have selected. Are they clear and easy to understand? Do you know exactly what each standard means? Can students and parents easily understand these standards? Possibly not.*

## Dividing Standards Into Components

You will need to break down your standards into what are called components, if the ones you're using are not already written that way. The process is most similar to outlining, breaking major headings into subheadings that explain and clarify the major heading. Components are the ingredients of the standard—the skills and knowledge that add up to the understanding of "big ideas," the major concepts that constitute standards. Or you may need to simplify standards that are too wordy, stripping them to their essence into clear, terse components.

**Components are the ingredients of the standard.**

## Understand the Need to Include Clear Components

Making sure standards include specific components that are clearly and simply written has a number of valuable uses:

- It explains and defines broadly stated standards.

- It allows you to focus instruction on one or more parts of a standard.

- It fosters clear communication with students and parents about what students will be learning.

- It helps you identify what students must learn in order to achieve the standard.

- It helps you write rubrics for performance assessment tasks more easily.

- It simplifies the job of writing standards-driven units.

## Clarify Standards

The idea is to outline each broad standard using straightforward language that anyone can clearly understand. Many of the national standards have already done this, and they need little further attention. Some standards, however, are so broad that they are unusable in their current state, and these standards need to be outlined into components. Other standards are highly specific and need to be stripped to their essence for this process.

**Outline each broad standard using straightforward language.**

Breaking standards into clear components answers the questions: What does it mean to use scientific inquiry to solve specific problems in real life situations? What will students have to learn in order to use scientific inquiry to solve real problems? What will have to be taught for students to use scientific inquiry to solve problems? Components answer these questions tersely—similar to an outline.

For good examples of how standards are already broken into specific components, look at National Council of Teachers of Mathematics (NCTM) Curriculum and Evaluation Standards for School Mathematics (Reston, Virginia:

NCTM, 1989). Those standards are "ready to go." Looking at how they are done will guide you, regardless of the subject matter you are interested in teaching. To see how components are varied for different age groups, look at Benchmarks for Science Literacy, in addition to NCTM.

Assess your selected standards to see which ones are already broken into components and which ones need to be expanded or clarified. There are basically three possibilities for the standards you have selected:

1. They are just fine as they are written.
2. They are too broad and need to be broken down into more detail.
3. They are too detailed or too technical and need to be simplified.

A music educator, for example, told an audience that students should be able to sustain a melodic line with the voice. A school board member asked, "Do you mean they can sing a song?" Write—plain and simple—so students and parents will know and understand exactly what each standard means. Students, parents, and ordinary folk should understand precisely and clearly what student standards are driving learning by looking at the components you write.

## Identify Standards That Are Complete

Some standards are already detailed, clear, and specific so that you, students, and parents know exactly what is included in the standard. Let's take another look at the NCTM standard from Step One (see left).

You know that students will explore statistics, and you know exactly what they will learn to do in the area of statistics. This standard is clear, and the broad area of statistics is already broken into components for you.

---

### Sample Math Standard from NCTM

In grades 5 through 8, the mathematics curriculum should include exploration of statistics in real-world situations so that the students can:

- systematically collect, organize, and describe data;

- construct, read, and interpret tables, charts, and graphs;

- make inferences and convincing arguments that are based on data analysis;

- evaluate arguments based on data analysis;

- develop an appreciation for statistical methods as powerful means for decision making.

---

## Identify Standards That Need More Detail

Compare that NCTM standard with the following example of a science standard, selected from Kentucky's Academic Expectations:

*Use scientific method to solve specific problems in real-life situations.*

This particular standard needs to be taken a step further by breaking it into the component parts that will have to be learned if students are to successfully "use scientific method to solve specific problems in real-life situations." Unlike the math standard from NCTM, this standard does not include the list of components that explains more specifically what the standard means. Before it can be used to drive instruction, it will have to be clarified.

For those standards that need clarification, list specific components under each broad standard by outlining what is included in the broad standard, using bullets to list the specifics that explain clearly what students will know and be able to do as part of each standard. Decide exactly what students will know and be able to do for each standard you have selected.

## Identify Standards That Need to Be Simplified

Finally, you may have to simplify some standards for use in this process. In Step Three you will be looking at large numbers of standards, with many cards spread out before you. You will need to be able to see quickly and clearly what each standard includes, so for the purposes of this process you may need to simplify highly detailed standards, stripping them to their essence. Otherwise, you will not be able to scan large numbers of standards with clarity or with speed. Look at this example of the standard for scientific inquiry from Benchmarks for Science Literacy (see page 32). Please understand that this is in no way critical of this standard or the way it is written. It is extremely clear and is ideal for most purposes, especially for instruction. It would be difficult to quickly scan large numbers of cards with standards written to this level of detail, however, and this particular standard needs to be stripped down and simplified for use in Step Three.

**For those standards that need clarification, list specific components under each broad standard by outlining what is included in the broad standard.**

## Scientific Inquiry

By the end of the fifth grade, students should know that:

- Scientific investigations may take many different forms, including observing what things are like or what is happening somewhere, collecting specimens for analysis, and doing experiments. Investigations can focus on physical, biological, and social questions.

- Results of scientific investigations are seldom exactly the same, but if the differences are large, it is important to try to figure out why. One reason for following directions carefully and for keeping records of one's work is to provide information on what might have caused the differences.

- Scientists' explanations about what happens in the world come partly from what they observe, partly from what they think. Sometimes scientists have different explanations for the same set of observations. That usually leads to their making more observations to resolve the differences.

- Scientists do not pay much attention to claims about how something they know about works unless the claims are backed up with evidence that can be confirmed and with logical argument.

## Your Turn! Step Two

*Instructions: Make sure each standard includes components that clearly define exactly what you want students to know and be able to do for each standard.*

1. List components for each standard, either expanding or simplifying each standard as necessary. NCTM standards are excellent examples, and California's Curriculum Frameworks and Guidelines and the Demonstrators in Kentucky's Transformations can be helpful here as examples. But any curriculum material you have that succinctly clarifies your broad standards will do the trick. (Textbooks can also serve as good examples of the process, since they have broad unit and chapter headings, with more specific subheadings in each chapter.)

2. Record each component on separate index cards and clip them to their appropriate standard cards.

3. Assign a number to each standard, and use that same number on each of the component cards that belong with that standard. Place the number in the top righthand portion of each card. This indexing will be essential when you start selecting the standards and components you will use in your unit.

---

### REMINDERS

- List standards selected for the year's teaching.

- Decide what each standard includes.

- Outline components for each standard.

- Write in plain English.

- Write standards, not activities.

# The Legbone's Connected to the Kneebone

*James has a friend named Alan, a really different kind of person who gave his mother many nights of lost sleep. He made a living searching for oil in unusual places and running a junk shop in Kansas, saving a brightly painted carousel horse to put on his oil well pump if he struck it rich.*

*More than fifteen years ago, Alan paid a Wyoming rancher for the exclusive right to search for dinosaur bones on his three-thousand-acre ranch. Friends chuckled, and his mother lost more sleep. Last year Alan organized a search party, and men in hard hats discovered bones. Big piles of bones. After carefully removing centuries of dust, Alan started making connections, putting the bones together day after day. When he finished, he had before him the largest Tyrannosaurus rex skeleton in the world! Value: ten million dollars. Cash. He sold it to Japan, paid on delivery. Connections made all the difference. And his mom finally got a good night's rest.*

## What You Will Learn in Step Three

1. Look at examples of strong connections among standards. Look at a wide variety of combinations of standards and learn to combine standards for improved instruction.

2. Make natural connections among standards within disciplines and then among standards between different disciplines, looking for matches that are natural and that enhance learning.

## Connecting Standards From Different Subjects

Making connections within and between subjects is your next step. What standards and components make the most sense together? What match will better help students know and be able to perform the identified standards? You are looking for connections that enhance learning.

For sake of simplicity, when we refer to making connections between standards and/or components of standards, we will simply use the term "standards" to refer to both, rather than "standards and/or components of standards." You may find yourself connecting broad standards with one another, connecting components with one another, and/or linking standards and components. Either way, you are connecting standards.

> You are looking for connections that enhance learning.

## Look at Examples of Connections Among Standards

Let's try looking at examples of connections that have the potential to enhance learning:

- Does your mathematics ask you to deal with data, perhaps statistics? Does that match naturally with scientific investigation?

- Are you looking at writing for different audiences in English/ language arts? Does that strike a chord with understanding the varying perspectives of different cultures in social studies ?

- Does the subject of patterns in mathematics suggest a search for rhyme patterns in poetry, or design patterns in pictures or sculpture, or rhythm patterns in music? What about patterns found in nature?

- Does using research tools to locate information blend with understanding democratic principles such as choice, freedom, and responsibility?

Follow the connections where they arise naturally. If they only seem to arise in two subjects, let them. If on the other hand there seem to be connections across even more subject areas, put those standards together. Either way, you've got the beginnings of a potential standards-driven unit.

Let's take a look at clusters of standards that are a natural fit. In science, students learn to identify and describe the earth as systems, to identify subsystems and components related to the structure of the earth. In social studies, they learn the structure of government as a system and apply the democratic principles they learn to real life situations. Systems! Systems in science. Systems in social studies. There's a good match!

In language arts, students use research tools with emphasis on technology, reading, writing, and public speaking. Why not read, write, research, speak, and manipulate data about systems of the earth and systems of government?

Think about problems like the use of fertilizers and pesticides on land, a problem that brings in both ecosystems and government. Use mathematical reasoning and statistical methods to organize mathematical information on the relationship between pollution of water systems and individuals' use of chemicals in and around their home, to use scientific inquiry to help develop proposals for maintaining or creating pure water. To write persuasively about their beliefs on the freedom of the individual vs. the health of society in relation to individual freedom and water quality.

**Doesn't it make more sense—to both students and adults—to actually use skills from language arts and math to develop concepts from science, social studies, and the arts?**

Doesn't it make more sense—to both students and adults—to actually use skills from language arts and math to develop concepts from science, social studies, and the arts? It's a natural mix.

## Make Natural Connections Among Standards

First, make connections within subjects. Look for standards that go hand in hand within each subject. Cluster standards in math, for example. Cluster standards in language arts or other subjects you have selected. A note of caution: Make only the connections that are "a must"—don't force a lot of connections at this point. Just the essentials.

Next, make connections across subjects. Then, once you have made connections within subjects, start to look across subjects for connections. Look at science and math together. Can you perform scientific experiments without manipulation of data? Look at social studies and language arts. Can you learn about U.S. government without reading and performing research? Be open to any possibilities. First, within subjects, make clusters where it makes sense to do so. Next, across subjects, make clusters where it makes sense to do so. Pay close attention to that "makes sense" stipulation! Only where it makes sense.

You will probably find yourself needing to use the same standard in more than one cluster or to use components more than once. That is no problem. Be flexible! If you find that you need to use a standard or component in two different clusters, simply make a second card. If you find that you need to divide component into something more specific, do it! Split it into two or more components if you need to. There are no hard and fast rules here. Just get blank cards, colored markers, and do whatever is necessary to make the connections work for you.

**Be flexible!**

Don't force the fit between standards! At first, you may find yourself trying to force the fit between standards in different subjects. DON'T! You aren't trying to make a full house or a royal flush. Don't match anything at all unless the connections are natural. The criterion is given at left.

Leaving standards out of a unit is not a sign of failure. The object is not to cover all standards in a unit, but to make sure that the standards are taught in ways so that all students can learn them. Some things will be

### Don't Force the Fit

Will working on these things together help students understand better than studying them separately? If the answer is "no," then don't make the connection. Nothing is gained by trying to make something fit—you will only get a bag of unconnected bones, not a skeleton. And you need a fully articulated skeleton on which to hang your standards-driven unit.

taught outside standards-driven units. You will have some standards that are not in the units, that stand alone. That's to be expected!

The focus in Step Three is on making natural connections among standards, NOT in giving major focus to connecting standards with activities. As you match different standards across subjects, however, you should play with broad ideas for instruction in order to know what is a natural fit. Some things just don't work together, some have limited options, and some—when you get it just right—make good sense and offer limitless possibilities for instruction and learning. In fact, when you find a really good fit, you will find yourself unable to think of the standards separately: "Why did we ever separate these standards in the first place? How could we have done that?"

Most ideas come out of science, social studies, and the arts. It is usually a natural match to hook standards focused on content (such as broad concepts and knowledge from different subjects) to standards focused on processing information (such as reading, writing, listening, talking, critical thinking, speaking, manipulating mathematically). Hooking ideas from science, social studies, and the arts to the processing skills necessary to gain new information, to manipulate that information, and to explain to others what has been learned is a natural way to learn. Is it possible to learn core concepts from science, mathematics, social studies, the arts, and humanities without processing information? Process and content are fundamentally intertwined and therefore make natural connections.

## Your Turn! Step Three

*Instructions: Connect learner standards (and/or components of standards) across subjects. Make connections only where working on these standards together will help students understand better than would studying them separately. Make connections both within subjects and across subjects.*

1. Place learner standards cards in front of you, with cards from each subject in separate horizontal rows (left to right). Place each component below the appropriate standard card so that you can see all cards (sort of like playing solitaire). If you color-coded your cards, the rows will look like broad stripes on a flag! Double-check to see that all standards and matching components are given a number so you can readily connect the standards and their components.

2. Sequence standards where necessary within each separate subject, basing your decision on essential prerequisites. Be open-minded, and sequence only what's essential. Sequence from left to right.

3. Cluster any standards that fit together within each subject. Hint: You will have many standards that stand alone if you have broadly stated standards. Don't expect to have everything clustered!

4.  Now try to connect standards across subjects for the best instructional fit. Try different combinations and discuss how instruction would make better sense to students with those combinations. Move, group, regroup, and cluster standards cards according to natural connections within and across subjects. Duplicate cards if necessary.

5.  Continue until you (or your group) have made the best connections possible for instruction. DON'T FORCE THE FIT! If the connection is not natural, let those standards remain alone.

6.  You will probably have some instances with all subjects integrated, some standards that may not be integrated, and all combinations in between. That's fine. There is no single correct way to do this!

7.  Mark your combinations of cards when you are finished (we use brightly colored removable sticker dots, in case we change our minds later) so you can remember what clusters of cards go together, clipping them together with paper clips when you store them.

8.  Your goal is to develop at least *one* good cluster of standards, a cluster that makes sense together and has potential for increasing learning, for developing a strong culminating task. One strong cluster. With experience, you will be able to identify several clusters and rough out potential units, but as a beginner you are interested only in selecting one naturally integrated cluster to use as the standards driving instruction and learning in your unit. Pick one.

---

### REMINDERS

•  Look for natural connections between subjects.

•  Think of possibilities for instruction as you look for the best fit.

•  Don't force the fit.

•  Keep the focus on helping all students achieve standards.

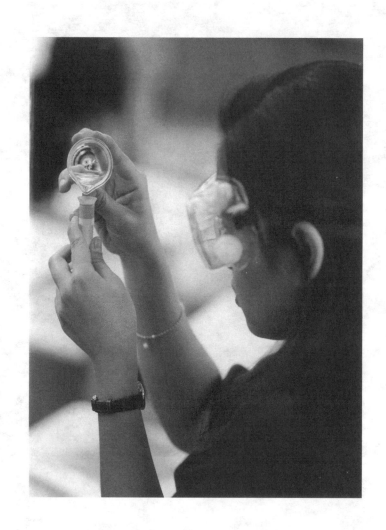

# The Real World

*The year is 1958. The place is Mr. Holifield's sixth grade classroom. Lee School. Desks are bolted in rows to an oiled wood floor. Washington and Lincoln gaze sternly down at the scene: thirty-five students working quietly in science books answering questions from the text—in complete sentences, of course.*

*The classroom is bare, except for a magical old glass bottle of litmus paper Becky found in Mr. Holifield's bottom drawer. She put it on top of his desk, but he never said anything about it. It just sat there. Pink paper, kind of brown around the edges.*

*The students used to sneak a piece from time to time and poke it in the dirt on the playground, trying everything they could think of to make it change colors. It never did.*

## What You Will Learn in Step Four

1. Understand what a culminating task is. Take a closer look at what a good culminating task is and how the culminating task embodies the standards selected for the unit.

2. Learn where to get ideas for culminating tasks. Culminating tasks answer driving questions. Learn sources of ideas for both driving questions and culminating tasks.

3. Develop a rough culminating task (or several different culminating tasks) for the cluster of standards you have selected.

## Developing the Culminating Task

You have before you clusters of standards that are a natural fit, that have the potential to work together to enhance instruction. Now what? You are now ready to learn how to energize your standards-driven unit by developing ideas for connections between "school stuff" and "the real world," ideas for real-world tasks that embody the standards and allow students to demonstrate mastery of them. We call this connection the "culminating task."

The culminating task makes the connection between standards and students—the real-world application that brings learning to life, that gives meaning and purpose to student work. This connection is the high-octane fuel for learning—kind of like those old "you're my reason for living" love songs. The culminating task. Every standards-driven unit has one. Remember the scene in *The Nutcracker* where the toys, frozen and still, come to life and dance—glittering and magical? The culminating task brings energy, life, and opportunity to your connected standards, just as the music brought the toys to life.

In Step Four, you will learn to collect ideas for tasks and will develop one or more rough drafts for culminating tasks for your unit. This is a difficult step, and you are going to have to read carefully in order to understand what you need to do. Developing a good culminating task is the heart and soul of your unit and of instruction.

**The culminating task makes the connection between standards and students.**

## Understand What a Culminating Task Is

The culminating task is the meaningful work students actually do to learn the standards, the driving force that unifies all the learner standards you have clustered together. It is a real-world activity, frequently called an "authentic task," that gives students a reason to achieve standards—an activity embodying the specific standards you have selected, the standards toward which all learning in your unit is directed.

The culminating task also serves as a way to measure student performance on these standards, allowing students to show that they have learned and are able to apply their newly acquired skills and knowledge. When you finish, the culminating task will totally embody the standards in your selected cluster of standards, and students will perform the standards by completing the task.

We need an extended definition here. In our case, the culminating task for our units is an event, a Pure Water Day organized by the students. Other kinds of culminating tasks could take many different forms, such as:

- A recommendation to a real governance committee or group

- The presentation of a student's own live play

- Defending positions in a debate

- Functioning in roles such as living history museum curators

- Becoming a governing body such as United Nations assembly

- Creating and implementing a solution to a real problem

The choices are limited only by your imagination!

Obviously, this is just the tip of the iceberg: The culminating task really encompasses the full unit and controls all activities that are part of the unit. The task involves all the learning sections and activities you saw in the sample unit in Part One, because all these activities in those sections move students toward successful preparation for the culminating task.

This complexity may seem a bit confusing at first, since educators have been used to teaching separated units of knowledge and then testing them separately. Think of it like real work.

Taking the culminating task as a goal for the standards-driven unit also helps students to prepare for the workplace, whether they're college-bound or intending to seek work directly after graduation. You are probably aware of the emphasis now being placed nationally on work readiness. It should make you feel highly productive to be killing two birds with one stone—helping students to achieve standards and teaching them workplace skills at the same time.

---

### Preparing Students for the Workplace

A culminating task is like an assignment in a workplace: The boss gives you a problem to solve and you have to go through several different tasks to provide the boss with a solution. There are natural questions that arise when faced with the task, concepts and information you must have and skills you must use to solve the problem. The work you are assigned determines what you must learn and then what you must do. You're going to be judged on the quality of the solution, with all the other work hidden from sight like the bottom two-thirds of the iceberg.

---

Let's look again at an example of a good culminating task taken from the sample unit in Part One, "This Land Is Your Land, This Land Is My Land!"

# THE CULMINATING TASK

*Students will plan, organize, and carry out for the community a Pure Water Day. The day's activities will focus on issues of water purity in the community. These activities will be designed to answer the driving question: Is the quality of our community's water affected by individual uses of land?*

As private citizens, we use a wide variety of chemicals in and around our homes, chemicals that have the potential to pollute the earth's water supplies. We use lawn fertilizer, pesticides, household chemicals, paint, thinner, motor oil, antifreeze, and many other common chemicals. We make frequent choices about how to use these chemicals, and we make choices about how to dispose of old or excess chemicals when we no longer need them. As individuals, our choices seem insignificant. Collectively, however, we may have a major impact—either positive or negative—on the community's water supply.

Your community is struggling with finding a balance between protecting personal freedom and protecting the water supply for the good of the entire community. How can a community protect its water supply from contamination by common chemicals (such as pesticides, fertilizer, paint, paint thinner, and motor oil) while maintaining individual citizens' rights to choose how they will use these chemicals in and around their homes and farms?

Your school has been asked to plan and implement Pure Water Day in order to present information and propose action about water purity in the community. As a result of your research and your proposals, you may persuade the community that water purity is in danger and regulations should be contemplated; or that the common water source is safe and no action is necessary; or that action may be needed in the future if present trends continue.

On Pure Water Day, you will design and present an informational exhibit for the public, including:

1. Models to show how water can become polluted by human activity through the water cycle.
2. An analysis of your community's opinions and practices in relation to pure water supply and use of chemicals, including charts and graphs to interpret data.
3. The results of scientific inquiry testing your hypothesis on proposed projects that will impact social attitudes and practices, based on information gathered in the public opinion poll.
4. A collection of editorials, published in newspaper format, presenting student opinions on the role of law and the U.S. Constitution in balancing personal freedom vs. community welfare, specifically related to water issues.
5. A presentation of your conclusions and your recommendations to the community for action. The project might be focused on ensuring the purity of water now or in the future, such as setting up collection points for discarded chemicals, paint, and motor oil; researching alternatives to chemical pesticides and fertilizers; or writing a children's book on the sources of water. Or your project might be focused on informing the public that there is not a problem. You should make your decision based on all the information you collected.

This is the culminating task. It is inseparable from its components: The students must keep Pure Water Day in mind as they move through each of the learning sections—the scientific experiments, the collection of data, the preparation of models for the exhibit, and so on. Each of these sections will be scored in the course of preparing for the task, so that individual students have grades and scores for their work. We'll discuss how each piece of work is scored in Step Seven. The point here is to understand how the culminating task drives the teaching and learning of standards and components.

## Learn Where to Get Ideas for Culminating Tasks

The culminating task begins with an idea. That idea might start as an essential question, as a problem to be solved or issue to be grappled with, as a project to be done.

How do you develop ideas for good culminating tasks? For the most part, you will be constructing culminating tasks from scratch or adapting what you find to fit your particular needs. You need ideas that you can use as springboards for developing culminating tasks. Ideas that can be merged, expanded, and shaped into robust culminating tasks that fit perfectly the different combinations of standards and components.

You need general ideas for connecting learner standards with real-world problems and real-world work, kickoff ideas that can grow (later!) into well-defined culminating tasks, ideas that can be fleshed out into reports, recommendations, presentations, problem-solving ventures—any number of tasks that can give life to a naturally connected chunk of learning.

Brainstorming is the only way to go. You begin to formulate hot ideas that act as bounceboards for other ideas. These ideas trip open all kinds of doorways and tend to evolve naturally into ideas for culminating tasks.

> You will be constructing culminating tasks from scratch or adapting what you find to fit your particular needs.

## Triggers

Where do you get these ideas? To get you started, there are lists of ideas in this step. But that won't be enough. Look for ideas as you read newspapers and magazines or watch television. Cut out articles and jot down ideas—questions, problems, projects—using the article as a source of rich ideas. File both the article and the ideas away for future reference. We call these ideas "triggers."

Triggers are not rigorous ideas—they're just what their name implies—something that sets off a train of thought. We use the word "trigger" to encourage you to keep a list of ideas to explore wherever you keep little notes—on paper scraps, on Post-it notes, on the computer. Then you have a store of ideas to draw on. But if you are the kind of person who doesn't keep notes or doesn't need triggers, fine. No compulsion here!

In a small Wisconsin school district, the teachers were looking for a culminating task that eighth graders should perform in their final year of middle school. A consultant asked the teachers, "What's the most talked about topic in your town now?" They answered, "Sidewalks. We've got a new high school and now we need sidewalks on some streets so that students can walk safely to school. But that means using tax money and taking over some private property; it's a big argument." The consultant said, "There's your eighth grade culminating task. Ask students to research the costs and the materials used for sidewalks, to find out what the opposing points of view are, and to make recommendations. You'll probably find differences in the recommendations, but if they are argued rigorously and are backed up with good reasoning and information, then they must be respected." This is an example of a trigger—one word: sidewalks.

Listen to your students talk to each other (probably the most productive source!). Listen to the questions they ask. What interests them? What are they curious about? What do they argue and feel passionately about, worry about? Turn their passions into interesting questions that will energize instruction and learning.

What are the "hot" local issues, the ones that may make you cringe just a little bit as you think about possible ruffling of local feathers? Use good judgment, but don't be afraid to put some life into learning—welcome to the "no pabulum" curriculum! This is your chance to break down that invisible barrier between school and the world outside.

Look at Kentucky's Transformations: Kentucky's Curriculum Frameworks (see Appendix A for ordering information). The charts in Transformations have performance assessment tasks that can be a tremendous source of ideas. Northern Illinois University, De Kalb, Illinois, has a Center for Problem Solving that has collections of ill-defined problems. Use Future Problem Solving team materials. *Horace's School* (Boston: Houghton Mifflin Co.), a 1992 book by Theodore Sizer, founder of the Coalition of Essential Schools, contains italicized examples of culminating tasks called "exhibitions." Workshops on performance assessments usually produce some promising ideas.

Frequently, ideas can't be taken over and applied to your situation without adaptation—you have to play with the ideas a bit and make them meaningful for you. But if you do find a good one, don't hesitate to adopt it wholesale. In education, stealing isn't a crime—it's creative acquisition. Life's too short to invent everything new.

> This is your chance to break down that invisible barrier between school and the world outside.

## Ideas for Driving Questions

One of the best ways to get ideas for culminating tasks is simply to brainstorm questions. Good questions inspire and demand good answers—they drive the answer and therefore drive the work. We call these "driving questions."

Every culminating task consists of some combination of the following: a driving question or series of questions and a problem to be solved or projects to be completed that will answer the driving questions. Think of the driving questions as pushing your entire unit toward the culminating task, which is one possible answer to them. For example, "Why did the Holocaust happen? Could it happen again?" might develop into a student-planned and student-implemented conference, with students from different schools participating in debates, presentations, theater and the arts, writing contests, and other appropriate activities.

Look at your standards-driven unit to see what questions could be answered by working on the standards you have clustered together. Look for

> Think of the driving questions as pushing your entire unit toward the culminating task.

questions that beg to be answered: questions that require students to explore and understand course content; questions that require students to use processing skills; questions that require students to learn new information, to critically analyze and combine new information with old and to think, to use both skills and content to answer them. Questions like "Why is there a high cancer rate in our county?" or "Is global warming real, and what difference does it make?" or "Do we need sidewalks?" Driving questions are fairly broad. Later they can be defined more narrowly and tailored to the needs of the specific situation. Here are some examples:

## Examples of Driving Questions

- What does it mean to be free in a democratic society?

- What natural disasters are most likely to occur in your area and how should the community prepare?

- What would happen if all bacteria and fungi were eliminated from earth?

- Is there life in outer space?

- Does history repeat itself?

- Is it worth the cost to explore outer space?

- Should Americans be required to have all of their usable body parts listed on a donor registry?

- If the sale of tobacco in the United States was banned, what types of replacement crops could be used to maintain the economy?

- Does the United States or the United Nations have the right or the responsibility to interfere in the internal affairs of foreign countries?

- Do labor unions still serve a useful purpose in the United States?

- If research shows that cigarette smoking kills people, why are we allowed to grow and buy it?

- Do the federal government or state governments have a responsibility to give financial assistance to people who have suffered losses due to major catastrophes (such as floods, hurricanes, and tornados)?

- With the Cold War over, should the U.S. military budget be cut or should the military be utilized for other duties?

- Should the U.S. government spend more money on preventing drugs from entering the country or on trying to cut the demand internally?

- Do governments have the right to execute citizens for attacks on the government and its policies?

- Should hanging be classified as cruel and unusual punishment?

- Is it true that men and women have more trouble communicating than men and men, or women and women?

- Is it possible to sustain the projected world population with present food production methods?

Let students brainstorm questions, and you will see where their interests really lie. Be prepared for some surprises! A group of teachers serving at-risk students was sure their students would only ask questions about "sex and cars." Yet, to their great surprise, the majority of questions concerned relationships, victimization, prejudice, and lack of control of circumstances that impact them. You will have much greater success at students achieving standards if you base instruction on questions STUDENTS are interested in, rather than on what WE are interested in, or (even worse) our best guess at what interests them. Throw the floor open and let kids—kids of all ages—in on this process! They will tell you.

## Ideas for Culminating Tasks

How do students answer driving questions and present solutions to problems? What form can their answers take? You are looking for projects that require students to know and perform standards. You are limited only by your imagination. Take a look at some examples.

- Hold debates between students and community organizations.

- Develop a United Nations conference with other local schools.

- Present an evening of student-written one-act plays.

- Write a newspaper editorial in Spanish.

- Exhibit personal portfolios.

- Display personal art exhibition in a public place.

- Work with a local animal shelter on a community service project.

- Debate individual rights vs. freedoms.

- Design a business that makes a profit.

- Prepare a newspaper from the 1850s.

- Develop an evacuation plan for a floodplain area.

- Determine and report on how much of each food group must be produced so that all persons on the earth would get their minimal daily requirements of each.

- Develop a system that would allow all Americans to be listed on an organ donor register and a system for the government to keep track of such a registry.

- Determine if it is feasible, in terms of population and economics, for people to not live on floodplains.

- Develop a partitioning of the former Yugoslavia to the satisfaction of the Serbs, Muslims, and Croats.

- Develop an advertisement campaign for two sides using a situation where there both sides are in disagreement.

- Develop a home-use hydroponics system to feed a family of four.

The ideas are out there. Once you get started you should have very little trouble either generating your own ideas or finding others—including students—who easily collect ideas galore.

## Developing Your Culminating Task

Now it's your turn to joint the fun! Select a cluster of standards that you think is naturally integrated, a cluster that makes you think of exciting ideas for student work. Then start to bounce back and forth between the cluster of standards and ideas for culminating tasks that require students to perform those standards, ideas that will help them learn the standards.

If working with colleagues, start with a rich, open, tolerant, risk-taking conversation. Stay tightly focused on the standards; brainstorm ideas for culminating tasks. Anyone who says too often, "We can't do that because" should be asked to hold the objection for later. This is a time to spin ideas!

Start to mix your ideas, connecting potential driving questions with possible projects or problems that answer the driving question, looking always at the standards to see that there is strong connection. Do this tentatively and expect to make lots of adjustments. You may have to discard all the ideas you have and look for a new set. You are looking for energizing, real-world connections that mirror the natural connections in standards. You are looking for tasks that are motivating to students. You are looking for tasks that require students to perform the standards, tasks that are measurable.

You will probably find that you also need to adjust the cluster of standards as you generate ideas for tasks. By thinking of real work, you will find connections among standards that were not obvious beforehand. Feel free to adjust the grouping of standards in addition to the task, as you learn from this process what is a good fit.

At this point in the process, you should be very freewheeling. It's fun! Don't hesitate to develop several different ideas for culminating tasks for

> Start to mix your ideas, connecting potential driving questions with possible projects or problems.

your cluster if you like. When you finish, you will have ideas for a driving question and culminating task that embodies your cluster of standards.

## Your Turn! Step Four

*Instructions: Develop ideas for culminating tasks that can be connected to clusters of standards. Select one or more ideas, including powerful driving questions that can be developed into a good culminating task.*

1.  Get more 4 x 6 cards and a different color of marker than you used before (or use smaller cards—you need an easy way to differentiate idea cards from standards cards). List a wide variety of ideas in the form of essential questions, projects, or problems that can be developed into culminating tasks, and write each idea on a separate card. Or cut out newspaper articles, collect video clips, select pieces of art. In short, use any source of ideas you can find.

2.  Match your clustered standards cards with ideas. Combine ideas or write new ones. You can regroup standards as you see new possibilities.

    Note: The advantage of doing the whole year at one time is that changing standards for one standards-driven unit affects the whole year.

3.  Record the your different ideas for driving question(s) and draft culminating tasks using the forms included at the end of the manual.

---

**REMINDERS**

*   The culminating task, when completed, needs to show student mastery of the selected standards.

*   Use natural connections.

*   Don't worry that you didn't get it right the first time—you will learn from your mistakes.

*   Collect many different ideas for tasks and save them.

*   Brainstorm! Don't reject any idea, no matter how crazy. You don't have to use it.

*   Ask the kids. You'll be surprised.

# The Final Culminating Task

*You've rented for years, spending hour after hour dreaming of building your own house. And now the time has come. Your time. The time to build. You have lists of things you require—two bathrooms, brick siding, a big kitchen with rocking chairs, a colonial herb garden, a lot with trees and a funny little slope right in the middle, and more. Picking just the right house plan is the key to it all.*

*You pick a style of house, look at your list, and start drawing floor plans on old grocery bags, moving back and forth between your list, the floor plan, and the style. Back and forth, round and round, making changes in each as you look for the perfect match.*

*Finally there it is. The perfect choice. You've got the plan. And with the right plan, you've got the right house. The house of your dreams.*

### What You Will Learn in Step Five

1. Map the content of your culminating task. By analyzing the direction your culminating task will move instruction, you can check to make sure it drives instruction toward selected standards.

2. Check the standards against your task. Learn to bounce between draft culminating task, your content map, and selected standards and their component parts to get a perfect fit for driving instruction with standards.

3. Check that you have a good culminating task. Learn the characteristics of a good culminating task, with questions to ask yourself about your own culminating task in order to finalize your work.

4. Finalize your culminating task. Use this information to finalize your culminating task for the unit you are writing.

## The Culminating Task Must Totally Embody the Standards

In fact, the task must be so good that you can remove the list of selected standards and the task will stand alone, reflecting all the selected standards in the very nature of the task itself. It must be totally tight. Every standard in the unit must be a necessary, natural part of the work of completing the culminating task. Every single standard.

The culminating task *replaces* the standards at this point, so it is critical that the task be a near-perfect match. The culminating task will now take over as the focal point for learning, as the way of measuring student achievement of standards, as the vehicle for student learning. The culminating task drives all instruction for the standards-driven unit. Picture the following algebraic equation:

$$\text{LEARNER STANDARDS} = \text{CULMINATING TASK}$$

It is your job to make sure the equation is equal, perfectly balanced. It is your job to develop a culminating task that naturally and clearly moves students toward successful performance on *all* the rigorous learner standards selected for the standards-driven unit.

> The culminating task replaces the standards at this point, so it is critical that the task be a near-perfect match.

## Map the Content of Your Culminating Task

Once you have a rough version of a culminating task, you need to take a close look at the direction that task will focus student learning. You need to make sure the task will direct student learning toward achievement of the selected standards. We call this process "mapping the culminating task." Let's take a look at a content map for "This Land Is Your Land, This Land Is My Land!"

Starting with a simple, terse summary of the culminating task, we chart the direction the task takes us by asking questions:

- What disciplines are involved in this task?

- What do students need to know within each discipline to complete the task?

---

### REMINDER

*What a good culminating task is not!*

Please stay awake on this one. Many thematic units you may have seen end in big showcase-style activities designed to let students share projects with parents, students, and others. The purpose of this type of activity is not *necessarily* to energize standards-based instruction or measure performance: It may simply be a sample of what students have done throughout the unit. Not good enough!

If the culminating task does not engage students directly in attaining standards, does not let you measure what students know and are able to do using all standards for the unit, then it is not a successful culminating task. No matter how exciting, it *MUST* allow students to achieve standards and teachers to measure student progress in reaching those standards if it is to be a good culminating task.

You end up with a picture of the possibilities for instruction in that task, a picture you can link with the standards to check for alignment. If you have a perfect match, you have a good task. If not, you begin adjusting until you are satisfied with the match. Let's look at a sample.

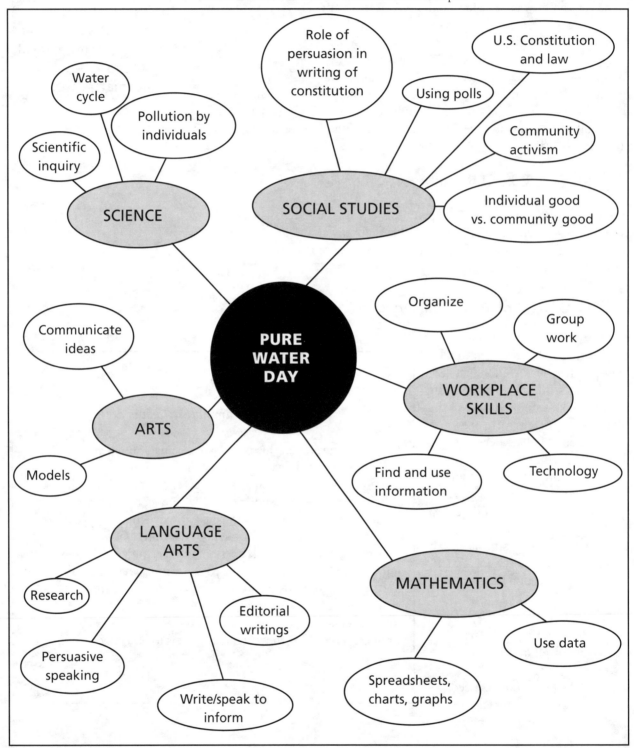

Graphic by Rebecca Frizzell

Very subtle shifts in the driving questions and culminating task can make a major difference in the work students will do and the focus of their learning—and therefore in the standards they will achieve.

In the sample unit on rights of the individual related to land use, consider the difference in social studies content when you work in the context of the United States as opposed to another country in the world: If you want students to learn about the U.S. Constitution, your task must set that as a parameter. What if you focus on pollution in the broader sense, rather than simply on water pollution? Will students then automatically learn about the water cycle, your selected standard, or is there a chance they might not focus on the water cycle at all? What if you have a debate rather than presenting Pure Water Day proposals? Will students then learn as much about community activism and the impact an individual can have? What if students write informational news stories rather than persuasive editorials? The standard changes. You focus students on achieving the standards you have selected by adapting and changing the task.

If your focus is on processing information and your content area standards are broad, you can develop a task that gives students wide choices in their variety of responses. If, however, you have narrow content standards, then you must write a more focused task.

## Check the Standards Against Your Task

You will go back and forth—over and over again—checking every standard and component against the requirements of the culminating task and the driving question. If students answer this driving question by performing the culminating task, will they achieve a particular standard? Does the task naturally lead students into the content you want them to know? Does it naturally lead them into achieving the standard? What about the next standard? And the next? Take a look at the following diagram:

**The Planning Process**

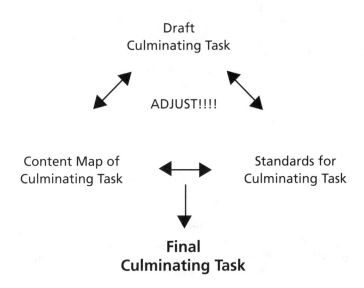

Draft
Culminating Task

ADJUST!!!!

Content Map of                          Standards for
Culminating Task                      Culminating Task

**Final
Culminating Task**

Back and forth. Round and round. Checking off each standard against the driving question and the culminating task. When the answer is "yes," that's a plus for the culminating task. If the answer is "no," then you will have to modify the culminating activity and/or the driving question. If you get a whole lot of "no" answers and only a few "yes" answers, then you probably do not have a good culminating task. Or you may not have a naturally connected cluster of standards, an integration that is natural and mirrors real work. If that happens, start over. Drag your idea cards out and go at it again.

*You are not finished working until you can answer "yes" to every standard and every selected component of the standards for your unit.* Until you know for sure that students will be able to successfully perform every single standard in order to successfully complete the robust, content-rich culminating task. Until you know for sure the culminating task leads naturally to what you want students to know and be able to do.

Actually these steps look great on a piece of paper, but the process and conversation won't be quite so lockstep. It's much more complex than it sounds, a circular, cyclical process—standards checking ideas, ideas connecting standards—that results in a crystal-clear culminating task, the driving force for learning. You will find yourself jumping around and doing all these things at once, looking for the best fit between standards and culminating tasks.

When you finish this process, you should know what is strong and you should know what needs attention. You should:

- Have an idea of whether or not your connections between standards are realistic.

- Know whether you have selected more—or fewer—standards than are realistic.

- Know if your culminating task is a natural match for the standards.

It is highly unlikely that you got it right first time. If you need to add some new standards, regroup standards, and rethink natural connections, take heart: It won't take you as long as it did the first time through.

It is possible, of course, that you got way off and have to start totally over. You should be able to make corrections by adjusting, but if you feel as if you have really gotten off course, don't be afraid to go back to Step One and start over. *You learn as much—if not more—from your mistakes as you do from your successes.*

> You learn as much—if not more—from your mistakes as you do from your successes.

## Check That You Have a Good Culminating Task

Once you have completed the process of adjusting the culminating task to match standards using content mapping, you have a final culminating task that has been through a rigorous process. Now you are ready to do a final analysis of that task before you move on. Here is a list of criteria to use:

### Do Students Learn Standards?

Does the task naturally and clearly move students toward successful performance on the rigorous learner standards you have selected for this unit? Will students be able to tell you exactly what they are learning? If it is a great activity but does not clearly and directly drive learning toward the clustered standards, drop it like a hot potato!

### Does the Task Provide an Answer to Your Driving Question?

Does the culminating task answer the driving question naturally? Does the connection make sense? Does it flow together for a single purpose?

### Does the Task Unify Standards Naturally?

Does the activity allow students to work in situations where different subjects are unified naturally? Is the task real or artificial? Does the instruction flow as a single unit rather than having fragmented, disjointed work that is connected loosely and unnaturally? Does the task make sense? Do the separate pieces flow together for a single purpose?

### Does the Task Motivate Students?

Would this subject interest students and make them excited about researching it? Perhaps even better: Is this something you could make interesting to most students? Is it a real problem or concern in the community where you live? Does it link students' lives and personal concerns with larger social issues and world concerns (ecological concerns, for example, that motivate many students these days)?

### Can You Measure Performance?

Will this task require students to demonstrate what they have learned? Can you measure their performance? Can you make decisions about instruction based on their level skill in completing the task?

### Are Local Resources Available?

Are there local resources—universities, business people, parents you know about, local natural features such as parks, rivers, lakes, mountains, architectural monuments—that make this idea appealing for students in your area and possible for you to teach? *Where possible, students need to learn from resources other than school and teacher.* What is available that you can use? This is not to suggest that only local ideas are good ones, but learning about where you live has clear built-in motivation and can serve as a good springboard for learning about your state, nation, and world. Are there school and community reference materials? Is technology available? What are the opportunities for hands-on work?

### Has Your Task a Form, Purpose, and Audience?

Will students know exactly what they have to produce—a report, a multimedia presentation, a recommendation to a committee—and who is intended to read/hear/view it? The task must result in a product that can be scored. It will be judged for its suitability for its audience and for the soundness of its content.

## Finalize Your Culminating Task

Continue to adapt the culminating task until it meets these criteria for success. A unique task depends on the natural connections among areas of learning and gives real direction for each particular standards-driven unit. Once you successfully connect your cluster of standards with a task, then the task *itself* guides you as you develop your unit. That is what is going to happen in the following steps of this manual—you will map your unit backward from the culminating task.

The culminating task is the most important part of your unit—actually it *is* the unit. It's worth your blood, sweat, and tears. Go for the gold!

## Your Turn! Step Five

*Instructions: Fully develop the culminating task for your unit. Make sure the task perfectly matches the standards and you know all the content required by the wording of the culminating task.*

1.  Select a draft culminating task. Place the task on a large table in front of you—or on the floor.

2.  Place your cluster of standards on the table (or floor) so that you can see all the standards driving your unit.

3.  Get several large, blank pieces of paper to do your content mapping. Start by drawing a circle in the center of the paper and writing a terse summary of your driving question/culminating task inside the circle. You might want to number the page so you can differentiate as you work through other drafts!

4.  Look at the draft culminating task, and map the content. Look for all the natural possibilities within that task as it is written. Be sure to take off your rose-colored glasses and see the task as it really is! You may have made assumptions that are not written into the task.

5.  Analyze the content map in relation to the selected standards. If you have a perfect fit, you can quit. Most likely, you will have to make adjustments over and over. Bounce between standards, content map, and culminating task until you have a perfectly aligned culminating task that embodies the standards. Continue to adjust the culminating task, analyze the altered task using the content map, and relate the task to standards until you have a product that is a perfect fit or until you decide to discard that draft culminating task and try another. You must have a task that embodies the standards, a task that will stand on its own when the list of standards is removed.

6.  Once you have a final culminating task, fill out the Checklist for Analyzing Culminating Task at the end of the manual. Analyze the culminating task you have written using the checklist. Decide if the culminating task is complete as is, if it can be successfully adapted, or—if the match is not satisfactory—if you need to start over on the culminating task. Evaluate your culminating task according to the criteria for a successful task. Make any necessary changes and finalize your culminating task accordingly.

---

**REMINDERS**

- The culminating task must totally embody the standards.

- Map the content to identify the learning potential for your idea, then shape the task to drive students learning the selected standards.

- Adjust until you have a near-perfect match.

- Use the checklist to help make improvements.

---

# Mapping Backward from the Culminating Task Into Learning Sections

*Christmas in a little shack way out West—the kids snuggled together in the cold, crisp evening, dreaming of a sugarplum morning.*

*The stories always say that they got an orange or tangerine in their stocking. Can you imagine how complicated it was to move an orange from an orange tree all the way to Kansas in 1869? If they did, a lot of people sure had to do a lot of planning.*

*Christmas morning, a tangerine in an old sock. One whole beautiful tangerine. Eaten section by incredible section. Can you imagine?*

### What You Will Learn in Step Six

1.  Learn to divide the culminating task into learning sections. Learn to think backward from the end result, asking yourself what chunks of work have to be accomplished in order to complete the culminating task.

2.  Learn to order the sections logically. Once you have decided the chunks of work that must be done, learn to order the work that needs to be accomplished.

3.  Backward map your culminating task. Apply what you have learned by backward mapping *your* culminating task into learning sections.

## Designing Your Unit

Now we're going to continue the planning for your unit. Because you have totally matched the culminating task with the standards for the unit, the task actually embodies the standards and you can now step back and put that task in the driver's seat. We are now going to talk about *mapping backward* from that task to the chunks of work that must be done, including all the skills and knowledge students will need to complete it well.

As you went through the process of matching the culminating task with the standards, you automatically began to think about everything students would have to do to perform the task, all the components of the culminating task. You began to think of what foundation concepts and skills students would need. You began to see how standards that reflect process and standards that reflect content mesh. You started to think about what resources students would need, what access to libraries and people and places were critical. Resources in your school and outside. Uses for technology to play a lead role in learning. Connections to careers and the world of work.

Now you will begin to see some natural sequencing, things that must be accomplished or understood before something else can happen. You start to see natural breaking points, stopping spots where it makes sense to assess student performance to see how students are doing on their journey. You start to see ways to use the results of those assessments to make changes in instruction, to provide extra help or additional challenge.

Even though you may not realize it, you are now on familiar turf. You are ready to start turning your culminating task into smaller sections of instruction. Think of the culminating task as the book, and now you have to divide it into units and chapters—pieces of the puzzle called "learning sections."

> You start to see natural breaking points, stopping spots where it makes sense to assess student performance to see how students are doing on their journey.

## Learn to Divide Culminating Task Into Learning Sections

Learning sections are large chunks of instruction that must be completed in order to accomplish the culminating task. For each section, you will know exactly what students will learn, how they will learn it, and how you will measure their success. The standards may be integrated or not, depending on each particular section: Some sections may be devoted just to a mathematics standard, or just to a science standard. Others may be integrated. The instruction will certainly vary, depending both on the task itself and the different needs of your students. The assessment—performance measured against standards—will be a natural part of instruction. All the work in each section adds up to the culminating task.

Break your task into learning sections based on the natural questions and the chunks of work that arise as students look at the culminating task. What questions are a natural part of the task? What separate pieces of work must be accomplished?

Learning sections, the building blocks of your unit, will eventually include more specific information:

1. Exactly what task students will complete by the end of teaching section (*where students are going*)

2.  Activities and instruction that facilitate student learning (*what students and teachers do to get students where they are going*)

3.  Rubric for evaluating student performance (*how you will score student work*)

But for Step Six your only task is to divide the culminating task into the major chunks of work that must be done in order to accomplish the task and the standards.

Let's take a closer look at the process so that you learn to break your unit into learning sections. Again, we'll use "This Land Is Your Land, This Land Is My Land!" for the example. You should be looking at the Culminating Task so you can see everything students must do to prepare for Pure Water Day.

You begin by writing a summary of the final activity students will be doing at the end of the unit, placing it in a box at the top of a blank page. Your first work will be rough, but that's okay. It might look something like this:

---

**Pure Water Day**

Students present proposals and exhibit water cycle models, public opinion data, scientific experiments, and editorials.

---

Look at the culminating task and see if anything is left out, if that is indeed what students have to do.

Now, ask yourself what must be done to do this, to have a Pure Water Day that includes proposals, water cycle models, summaries of public opinion, student editorials, and science exhibits. Don't worry about the order at this point, just try to identify the big chunks of work and put each separate chunk of work in separate place on the rest of the page. It might be neat, it might be pretty sloppy—depending on how you like to work. The main thing is to see what work has to be done. It might look like this (see page 69):

**PURE WATER DAY**
Present to the public
proposals, water cycle models, public opinion poll,
scientific experiments, editorials

*Prepare for Pure Water Day*
Organize, get facility, invite
public, budget

*Editorials*
Learn to write persuasively,
base opinions on U.S. Constitution, research knowledge
of water cycle and public
opinion poll

How does water get polluted?
Learn about *water cycle and
relation to individual use of
chemicals,* make models
demonstrated

Develop and present *proposal
for maintaining or improving
water quality*

*What does the public think?*
What do they do? Poll public and
information to get ideas for proposal; test idea, using scientific
inquiry first

*Scientific inquiry*
Use to test idea for proposal
based on opinion poll and
research

Graphic by Rebecca Frizzell

We now have the final event at the top and chunks of work that students must do to be ready for the final event place all over the page in no particular order.

## Learn to Order the Sections Logically

Look at the culminating task in the sample unit and consider what we have asked students to do as part of the unit. Does it matter what the order is? Would it make sense to develop proposals for projects without first collecting information, without understanding the water cycle and its relation to pollution, without knowing what the community actually believes and practices? To use scientific inquiry to determine what projects might impact social attitudes and practices without knowing what those attitudes and practices are? Would it make sense to present Pure Water Day to the public without organization and preparation?

Clearly the order does matter. *There are always foundation skills and concepts students must know to be able to complete the culminating task.* Do students know how to use the computer for spreadsheets, graphs, and charts? Do they understand the continuum from "pure" to "polluted" water? Have they learned to use the scientific method? Considering what students need to know in order to take the next step will begin to determine naturally the sequence of the unit for you.

There is one final thing to do—decide the appropriate order of the work. Basically, we have two choices: (1) We have some things that must be accomplished as a foundation for other work, things that must be done sequentially, or (2) we have work that can be done simultaneously or that can be done alone. We move the sections around, either by giving the sections numbers or by getting a new piece of paper and putting them into a rough flowchart showing what needs to be done first, what can be done at the same time. Once we have made a final decision, we complete the task by putting the sections into final form: the flowchart.

The whole focus is on backward mapping from the final event. Therefore, we start at the top with the final event and work our way backward from that point, moving farther and farther down the page until we finally reach the beginning of the unit, the foundation, the part that must come first if students are to move successfully toward completion of the culminating task.

Let's take a look at "This Land Is Your Land, This Land Is My Land!" and see. The example is a flowchart, and the final activity is at the top of the page, and work students must do initially begins at the bottom of the page. Students will work their way from the beginning of the unit (at the bottom of the page) to the final activity (at the top of the page). It looks this way because it is a backward mapping document, a tool for planning the unit, a teacher perspective of the unit. Everything flows backward, is planned backward, from the end activity, the culminating task. The sections are numbered for identification, not necessarily for sequencing. Learning sections that are occurring at the same time are side by side, with students beginning the unit with Sections One and Two, moving on to Sections Three and Four, then with Sections Five and Six, and finally with Pure Water Day.

> There are always foundation skills and concepts students must know to be able to complete the culminating task.

## Unit Broken Into Learning Sections

---

**Pure Water Day: A Community Exhibition**
(Math/Science/Language Arts/Social Studies/Art/Technology)

Present informational exhibition for the public, including models of water cycle, analysis of public opinion and practices, and results of scientific inquiry exploring proposed projects that will impact social attitudes and practices, and proposals for action that will inform the community that there is not a problem or that will prevent or correct a problem now or in the future.

↑                                                    ↑

---

**Learning Section 5**
(All teachers)
Plan for implementation of Pure Water Day.

**Learning Section 6**
(All teachers)
Prepare for project based on information you have collected and present on Pure Water Day.

↑                                                    ↑

---

**Learning Section 3**
Inquiry
(Math/science)
Use scientific inquiry to form and test hypothesis on proposal for projects that will impact social attitudes and practices identified in public opinion poll.

**Learning Section 4**
Scientific Student Editorials
(Language Arts/Social Studies)
Present opinions on the role of law and the U.S. Constitution in balancing personal freedom vs. community welfare, specifically related to water issues.

↑                                                    ↑

---

**Learning Section 1**
Public Opinion Poll
(Math/language arts/social studies/technology)
Develop poll to measure public opinion, knowledge, and practices. Collect and interpret data, presenting conclusions with charts and graphs.

**Learning Section 2**
Water Cycle Models
(Science/Art)
Learn about water cycle and how it gets polluted using models.

## Backward Map Your Culminating Task Into Learning Sections

Now it's back to the salt mines! Read over your culminating task, identifying the natural chunks of work that will have to be done to accomplish the task, what students need to know and do to learn and perform the standards. Look for the natural order of the work. Picture writing your family tree, beginning with you. You start with the end product and branch backward from that final product. It's easiest to use a flowchart like ours, starting with the end and working backward as you plan the learning sections, then implementing the unit beginning at the bottom of the page and working your way up to the final activity. Think about your culminating task and what is included. Then work your way back through the task, beginning at the end. Just keep falling backward—it's as easy as falling off a log!

## Your Turn! Step Six

*Instructions: Divide your standards-driven unit into learning sections. Base all your decisions on the culminating task: Begin with the task and move backward.*

1. Ask yourself these questions: "What do students need to do to complete the culminating task? What do students need to do to learn the standards and components being addressed?" Look for questions that flow naturally out of the task. Use both your content map and these questions to look for the natural chunks of instruction necessary to complete the task and have students achieve standards. Get a big sheet of paper and summarize the final task, then start drawing chunks as a visual, showing the work that must flow into the final task.

2. Once you have divided the culminating task into chunks, you have identified your learning sections. These sections might either produce a thing (like the opinion survey), knowledge of new concepts, or new ability to apply skills.

3. Finally, decide the order in which the learning sections must occur for optimal learning. You will find that there are many choices, with some things that must be done sequentially and others where the work is somewhat independent. Give it your best shot, and you can always adjust later as you develop the instruction more specifically.

---

### REMINDERS

- Keep standards in mind—always!

- Keep cycling back between the culminating task and the standards.

# Rubrics and Scoring

*It's early spring, and the rookies are gathering at their training camp for more grueling practice. They run long distances, work out with weights, watch films, practice batting and catching. They clean their uniforms. They learn to work as a team. They go to bed early—bone-weary—and then get up and do it again.*

*Day after day, they practice and practice and practice. Just why do you think they do that? Would they do all that work if there were no opening day at the ball park, no umpire yelling "Play Ball!"?*

*Would they practice hard if no one kept score, if there were no World Series?*

## What You Will Learn in Step Seven

1.  Learn about performance assessment. Learn how performance assessment differs from traditional assessment, and the different types of performance assessment.

2.  Learn how to score performance assessment. Scoring performance assessment is done by using rubrics.

3.  Learn how rubrics are constructed. Learn how to construct rubrics, step by step.

4.  Learn how to use rubrics or benchmarking. Learn to find benchmark papers to use with rubrics.

5.  Look at examples of rubrics. See samples of rubrics used for our theme unit.

6.  Write rubrics for your unit. Using the information in Step Seven, construct the initial rubrics for your unit.

You're very close to having a unit ready for a trial run. You have a culminating task giving definition to what students will actually be doing, how they will be learning the standards, how they will perform what they have learned. You've divided it into teaching sections, and you know roughly the order in which students will complete their work. But you don't yet know how you're going to score it.

You are going to score student work using a new form of assessment called "performance assessment." Let's take a short breather here and get a little background about this new form of assessment. While it seems quite complex at first glance, the philosophy is quite simple: Students demonstrate they can use what they have learned, and you score their work, using a scoring guide called a "rubric" to see if is up to snuff when compared to examples of good work. Let's look first at understanding performance assessment.

## Learn About Performance Assessment

In the olden days—actually not so very long ago—taking a test was something everyone understood. The test might include any combination of multiple-choice, fill-in-the-blanks, matching, true-false, short-answer, and the dreaded essay questions. You had a test at the end of each chapter in the textbook, and you had comprehensive tests at the end of each unit, possibly at the end of each semester. That was it. Pretty simple, wasn't it?

The problem with this type of assessment was that it did not require students to use in a meaningful way what they learned. Many students, therefore, learned just enough to pass the test and no more. Passing the test was often a matter of memorizing large volumes of material, skimming the surface rather than probing the depths. The author John Holt wrote in his famous book, *How Children Fail,* "The major difference between the good student and the poor one is that the poor student forgets right away while the good one is careful to wait until after the examination." Not good enough for the information age! Students must now take their learning another step forward: They must apply what they have learned.

If the old tests required memorizing masses of material, and we are not primarily interested in having students continue to do that, how can we refocus on performance? Change the test! Pay attention to the age old question students ask again and again, "Is this going to be on the test?" If so, the students themselves certainly pay attention!

Assessment and learning are inseparable. If we want students to change and to apply what they learn, then it makes sense to change the requirements of their tests. And that's exactly what is happening. The tests are changing.

Let's review some terms. New forms of assessment are often referred to as *performance, authentic, alternative, or performance-based assessment,* because they require students to perform real work by completing authentic tasks that simulate real world events. It doesn't really matter what you call it. It does matter that you understand that we're NOT talking about multiple-choice, norm-referenced tests. The word "assessment" is usually used to distinguish measuring performance from traditional testing, but we won't be compulsive about terminology.

Students demonstrate they can use what they have learned, and you score their work, using a scoring guide called a "rubric."

Assessment and learning are inseparable.

*Performance assessment* is a different kind of assessment in which students must use what they have learned and demonstrate mastery of world-class standards. Performance assessment is the measure of whether or not—and to what degree—students achieve the standards. Performance assessment is also referred to as authentic, alternative, or performance-based assessment—all direct demonstrations of skill and knowledge. It *replaces* multiple-choice and short-answer tests—you shouldn't use them together, and you'll find you can't because they reflect different kinds of teaching.

Performance assessment (our preferred term) requires students to respond with their own words or constructions to questions or prompts involving complex tasks rather than selecting preconstructed answers. When a student answers with their own words and ideas, these are called "constructed-response questions."

Performance assessment is not one genre. Although we will list the major kinds below, you shouldn't believe that this is an exhaustive catalog: Anything that can be judged—and therefore scored—can be used as a performance assessment. Socratic seminars, for example, have been used as an assessment tool: Judges sit around the outside of the discussion circle and score the leader and the participants on the quality and quantity of their contributions.

Performance assessments come in two major types:

1. *On-demand assessments:* The response to a question or "prompt" happens at a certain fixed time and place. You're familiar with on-demand because standardized testing is on-demand, but students won't be filling in bubbles with #2 pencils—they'll be explaining, perhaps orally or perhaps written, or justifying a decision, or applying their knowledge to a new situation.

2. *Curriculum-embedded assessments* happen exactly as their name implies—during the curriculum. Curriculum-embedded assessment is not separated in time and place from normal classroom activity, and that fact may be difficult to understand. How can you teach students and assess them at the same time? If you think about it, you do this routinely, judging where a child is and what would be the appropriate next steps for this child. Curriculum-embedded assessment just makes a natural teaching process available for others to see, including the students themselves.

Probably the best-known curriculum-embedded assessment is the *portfolio*, which presents a selection of work to demonstrate an important aspect of learning—ability to write in four or five genres, for example, or the development of a science experiment with explanations for all the choices made. But curriculum-embedded assessment also includes extended projects such as New Standards Project's capstone projects; group projects; and the collections of work called "exhibitions," pretty much like the bundle of work culminating our sample unit.

Portfolios are selections (*not* just collections) of student work gathered to demonstrate achievement in learning. They may include constructed response assessments as part of the evidence of achievement, although portfolio contents are not limited to any single kind of components. Portfolios are constructed over time and must have a purpose clearly understood in advance by teacher and student.

Exhibitions can be portfolios, but they are usually broader collections of work required for a special purpose, such as for graduation from a Coalition of Essential Schools high school. In our case, the culminating task is often an exhibition, meaning a public presentation of results that includes different forms of evidence supporting a conclusion. Or it might be an activity in which students must use what they have learned, such as defending a position in a debate or functioning in roles such as living history museum or becoming a governing body such as United Nations assembly. And yes, they can all be scored. Let's take a look and see how.

## Learn How Performance Assessments Are Scored

Scoring sessions are guided by *rubrics*—scoring guides developed for each individual task or classes of tasks. Rubrics describe the features student products are expected to include for each specific score. There is a chosen scale, with a range of choices for scoring student performance. Why the term "rubric"? It derives from the Latin word for red, and refers to directions printed in red letters in Christian liturgical books prescribing the order of the service.

Rubrics make the bridge between the standards and the assessments. If students must be able to write a variety of genres for different audiences, then the rubric must focus on the required genres and the descriptors of the level of performance required for each score.

Please note that it doesn't matter what the *curriculum* required the students to do: Provided they learned how to write memos, for example, it doesn't matter whether they are memos recommending the purchase of a software package or memos summarizing the views of water quality-control experts. *It only matters that the students meet the standards: writing memos.*

Obviously you can't use a machine to score performance assessments. Instead, they are usually scored by groups of "raters," "scorers," or "readers," who look at all the products and agree on a score. It's a long, difficult process which is also thoroughly exciting and gives unique insight into the process of teaching and learning. You will get some experience in this arena as you complete your unit.

> Performance assessments are usually scored by groups of "raters," "scorers," or "readers," who look at all the products and agree on a score.

## Learn How Rubrics Are Constructed

In some instances you can use rubrics that are already developed, or you may find pieces of existing rubric charts that will suit your needs if combined. But, for the most part, you will need to develop your own rubrics for analyzing student performance. *Constructing rubrics* is not really hard, although you will find that rubrics need continual adjustment in their wording as you begin to use them.

1. Choose a scale along which you will place student work. You can use a four-point scale (4, 3, 2, 1) or a six-point scale (6, 5 4, 3, 2, 1). In Kentucky, the points on the scale are labeled: *distinguished, proficient, apprentice,* and *novice.* It's a good idea to have an even number of points, so that scorers are forced into making a judgment of quality. If there is a middle point, too many scorers will hedge by giving the middle score for safety.

2. Imagine the best possible response to the task at hand. Describe this best response. Don't worry about whether students will be able to produce it—just describe it. *Use the language of the standards.* The standard is the top level of your rubric.

3. Describe a slightly less-accomplished response for the next score down, and so on. Use words that indicate a scale: "always," "sometimes," "occasionally," "never," or "consistent," "not quite consistent," "patchy," "inconsistent."

4. Make a breakpoint on the scale between:

   • Responses that just need some assistance in order to reach the standard (4–3 OR 6–5–4 OR distinguished, proficient)

   • Responses that demonstrate the need for reteaching (2–1 OR 3–2–1 OR apprentice, novice)

5. Let students see the rubric at *the beginning* of the learning section, so it will guide their performance as they work, with no surprises at assessment time.

### Learn How to Use Rubrics, or Benchmarking

You are going to learn how to use rubrics to score student work, a process that is also called "benchmarking." However, because you are still in the process of constructing your unit, you won't actually be able to do this for yourself right now. You don't have any student work to score! This work will be done after you have completed teaching your unit, when you have student work in hand. At this point, we will simply show you what to do.

**What If the Work Is Not Complete?**

Rubrics shouldn't talk about missing pieces of work. There should be no counting of items in the portfolio here. If the work is not complete, the portfolio or exhibition is not scored. Bear in mind that employers can't afford to give extra time when employees don't do the job. Standards-driven instruction assumes that the student completes all the work.

An important preliminary point about using rubrics and scoring is that the focus is on quality of the overall work, not on completion of assignments.

To look at student work, you need to work in groups of about four or five. You may be all teachers, but as you get more sophisticated, bring in a parent, an administrator, a business person, even a student. The discussions you will have with your scoring (rating or reading) group will be about quality, about your expectations, about the differences between what you taught and what students learned. Experiencing what students have produced gives teachers insight into their jobs and also motivates them to try new ways of teaching—as no other experience can.

The intention is to score all the student work, but you begin by finding what are called "anchor papers," or benchmark papers. These are examples of the score points on your scale, examples of each number (6, 5, 4, 3, 2, 1 OR 4, 3, 2, 1 OR highest, next-to-highest, next-to-lowest, lowest OR whatever scale you choose). Here's the step-by-step process for selecting benchmark work:

1. Try to find examples from student work for each point on the scale. You may not be able to find examples of the top (best) score or even the second-best.

2. Discuss the qualities of these anchor products with the group of scorers until everyone can recognize them. This can take more than half of the time allotted for scoring—but it's worth it.

3. Be prepared to modify the rubric if it clearly isn't working, but DON'T adjust it to produce a normal curve. Remember those standards!

This last point is hard to accept and harder still to practice. We're so used to giving the best paper in the class an "A" that we have to be continually reminded that the standard must be reached if the top score is to be earned. The best product in the class may only be a "next-to-highest score." Students (and their parents!) will find it hard to understand that some classes will not have any work earning the top score. It is also possible to have a class in which almost everyone earns the highest score, because successful teaching and learning brings ALL students to the standards.

Everyone needs to agree on how to handle protests from students, administrators, and parents about standards-driven scoring. And of course, you yourself need to be convinced so that you can be convincing when you explain. You will certainly be more convincing after you've been through all the steps in this manual and heard enough about standards to last the rest of your life!

**It is possible to have a class in which almost everyone earns the highest score, because successful teaching and learning brings all students to standards.**

## Look at Examples of Rubrics

We're going to show you a couple of rubrics from the sample unit we are using throughout this manual. First we'll list the task for the particular learning section, followed by the standards and the components being addressed in that section, and then finally show the rubric for measuring how well students meet those standards. Look closely at the link between the standards and the rubric—the rubric must reflect all the selected standards, focusing student attention on successfully learning and performing every standard. The standards, the task, and the rubric should be synchronized. Let's take a look at an example.

## Learning Section One: Public Opinion Poll

### *The Task for Public Opinion Poll*

Develop an instrument and process for measuring public opinion concerning the local community's understanding of the issues regarding individual use of chemicals and the purity of water supply and their practices. What does the community know, what do they think, and what do they actually do? Collect and interpret data, including use of charts and graphs for clarity, so that the public can understand clearly what you find.

### *Standards and Components for Public Opinion Poll*

#### Mathematics

- Students understand and accurately use statistics and probabilities.

    - *systematically collect, organize, and describe data*
    - *construct, read, and interpret tables, charts, and graphs*
    - *make inferences and convincing arguments that are based on data analysis*
    - *evaluate arguments based on data analysis*
    - *develop an appreciation for statistical methods as powerful means for decision making.*

#### Language Arts

- Students read a wide variety of material, including technical information needed to complete projects.

    - *know jargon and specialized language used in mathematics, social studies, science, and technology*

- Students speak and write to communicate information and ideas to various audiences for various purposes.

    - *write and speak to persuade*
    - *write and speak to inform*

#### Workplace Skills

- Students can find and use the information they need to meet specific demands, explore interests, or solve specific problems.

#### Social Studies

- Students observe, analyze, and interpret human behaviors to acquire a better understanding of self, others, and human relationships.

*The Rubric for Public Opinion Poll*

**Highest score**

The results show a total understanding and accuracy of student use of collecting and organizing data and in constructing charts and graphs that reflect the data. There is complete understanding of the issues involved in ways to gather information about human behavior. The student has understood what information was needed and has skillfully crafted questions to get at this information. The display of data is entirely appropriate and completely persuasive.

**Next-to-highest score**

The results show a good understanding and overall accuracy of student use of collecting and organizing data and in constructing charts and graphs that reflect the data. There is general understanding of the issues involved in ways to gather information about human behavior. The student has understood what information was needed by reading a wide variety of material and using specialized language, understanding how to craft questions to get at this information. The display of data is appropriate and persuasive.

**Next-to-lowest score**

The work shows patchy, inconsistent understanding of the systematic collection, organization, and description of data. Some of the issues are understood, but some of the questions are less focused than others. The student's ability to find information and convey results is sometimes clear, but not always.

**Lowest score**

The work shows little or no understanding of the systematic collection, organization, and description of data. One or two of the issues are understood to a limited degree, and the questions are unfocused and specialized language is incorrect or not present. There is little evidence of the student's ability to understand and use data.

\*    \*    \*

You should see a direct tie between the rubric and the task, so that students know clearly how their work and their achievement will be scored. You should also see a direct tie between the rubric and the standards, and between the standards and the task. Let's take look at one more example.

## Learning Section Two: The Water Cycle

*The Task*

How does the water cycle work? Design a model explaining how water is produced and how it gets polluted. The model must communicate clearly and accurately how the water cycle works, and exactly how water can be polluted by the use and disposal of chemicals on the earth's surface.

*Standards and Components for Learning Section Two*

**Science**

- Students complete tasks and create products that identify systems and components and the ways the parts work together.

    – *understand water cycle*
    – *understand interaction between water cycle and pollutants on earth's surface*
    – *know basic facts about the toxicity of certain chemical compounds*

- Students demonstrate understanding of the effects of human activity on the environment.

**The Arts**

- Students use knowledge of the principles of design to communicate ideas clearly.

*Rubric for Learning Section Two*

**Highest score**

The display shows not only a complete understanding of the water cycle and what can make it toxic through human activity, but also a mastery of the principles of design.

**Next-to-highest score**

The work shows an understanding of the water cycle and how it can become toxic through human activity. The visual display is competent, but not inspired.

**Next-to-lowest score**

The work shows some understanding of the water cycle and how it can become toxic through human activity, but the understanding is not consistent and the display may reveal incomplete understanding of the system.

**Lowest score**

The work shows little or no understanding of the water cycle and how it can become toxic, and the visual display does not communicate how the system works.

\*   \*   \*

These are just two of the rubrics needed for the complete unit, "This Land Is Your Land, This Land Is My Land!" There are six learning sections in this particular unit, and they each have a rubric. You can see them all, complete with detailed information on instruction, by looking at the completed unit in Step Nine.

You can see how giving students the rubric at the beginning of each learning section can focus their attention on successful performance of standards.

You can see how the rubric itself becomes a tool for learning, not simply a measure of success. In addition, writing rubrics forces us to articulate exactly what students must do in order to be measured as successful and focuses us on driving instruction with the standards rather than with activities.

### Write Rubrics for Your Unit

Finally you are ready to go to work, to write the rubrics that will be used to score each learning section in your unit. Go back in this section to the step-by-step directions for how to write rubrics, then use those directions to jump right in and give it a try. Stick close to your selected standards, and you'll have it made!

## Your Turn! Step Seven

*Instructions: Write the rubrics for your unit, developing a rubric for each separate chunk of instruction you will be scoring. Be sure the rubric matches the selected standards and the task.*

1. Choose a scale along which you will place student work, probably a four- or six-point scale. Use an even number so there will be no midpoint.

2. Look at the standards you want students to attain in each learning section. Use the language of the standards to design a rubric ranging from the best possible performance to the least successful performance.

3. Decide the breaking point on the scale that indicates successful performance (or performance that requires minor assistance) and performance that demonstrates the need for reteaching.

4. When the unit is underway, you will finalize the rubric by trying it out on some pieces of work in progress and adjusting it.

5. After the each learning section is complete, organize a group of scorers and set aside a block of time to identify benchmark papers for each point on your scale, and then to score the students' work for that learning section.

---

### REMINDERS

- Keep your eye on the standards as you write the rubrics.
- Make clear to the students how their work is going to be evaluated.
- Be prepared to explain and defend performance assessment and scoring by rubric.
- Make it clear that you will NOT score incomplete work.
- Show the rubric to the students as soon as you're confident with it.

# Polishing the Stone

*It was 1969, and we were just out of college, eager to change the world. We were living in Chicago, teaching mentally handicapped teens to live in this new world we would create. We decided they needed to learn how to work, and the kitchen seemed a lovely starting place. Mary, the elderly cook, would love our help!*

*Francis had been in an institution for years and did very little. He sat mostly, seeming uninterested in all the stimulating things we paraded before him. For some unknown reason, we decided Francis could dry silverware. And—miracle of miracles—he did! The spoons shined, polished to perfection, stacked in perfect order ready for the morrow. Francis was working! Our program was working! Success at last!*

*Mary whispered and motioned to us to take a peek, without disturbing the work. There stood Francis, surrounded by piles of shining spoons, working on one more spoon for the pile. He very carefully, ever so slowly, lifted the spoon to his lips and gently blew warm air over the surface, just enough to get it nicely moist. Then he dried the spoon on the tail of his old red T-shirt, stacking the polished spoon carefully on top of a stack.*

*Francis polished the spoons, and Mary polished Francis. With just the right touch. Thank goodness for Mary.*

## What You Will Learn in Step Eight

1.  What instructional strategies are best? Review the wide variety of teaching strategies at your fingertips, focusing on the best uses for each particular strategy.

2.  How long should the unit be? Discuss thoughts on the length of your unit.

3.  How does flexible scheduling work? Take a look at how making decisions about scheduling based on the work being done can enhance learning.

4.  What about flexible grouping? Look at being able to group and regroup students for maximum impact.

5.  What about resources and materials? Think of the many resources and materials available.

6.  Look at an example of a completed learning section. Take a look at a completed learning section so you can see what is included.

7.  Think about the order of learning. Think about how students actually learn skills in the context of real work.

8.  Finalize your unit.

Let's take stock of where we are now. You have a culminating task tied tightly to the standards selected for your unit. You have identified learning sections, the large chunks of instruction, and have sequenced those learning sections logically. You have written rubrics to use for scoring. Now it's time to backward map each learning section, to break each learning section into more specific plans for implementation, and to look again at teaching and what it means in standards-driven learning.

## What Instructional Strategies Are Best?

Before you can successfully break your learning sections into more detail, you need to think about the vast repertoire of teaching skills available for you to draw from.

Instructional strategies tend to follow fads. We were all taught by the lecture method: That's why classrooms are designed with a blackboard at one end and desks all facing toward it. That fell into disfavor and student-centered strategies took over: We all had to use cooperative groups and we got used to the "jigsaw" and the jargon of cooperative learning. We switched from basals to whole language and reading literature; discovery learning and hands-on learning also came in, along with the Madeline Hunter method (from another angle); and Socratic or Paideia seminars took hold.

If you're a teacher who's been around a while, you have learned a number of excellent methods of teaching just by catching each fad as it arrived, took over, and then receded. And now, thanks to each fad, you have a vast reservoir of strategies at your disposal!

As a teacher, you will need to exploit your repertoire of instructional strategies—your ways of teaching—and adapt your strategies fluidly to the kind of knowledge and skills you want to develop in the students. If you can adapt your teaching style to use any or ALL of these strategies, then you're in a great position to be flexible. *To teach standards-driven units, you need a wide variety of strategies, each adapted to what students are learning.*

No single teaching strategy is good or bad as such—it is either useful or not useful according to the outcome and to the students' own abilities and knowledge. The trick is to match the strategy to the needs, both of the subject matter and the students. Socratic seminars, for example, are better suited to understanding a historical or literary text than to designing a scientific experiment.

Students, like all the rest of us, have both different learning styles and different kinds of intelligence. Since it is not practical to match teacher and student learning styles for every teacher and every student, we should allow for the maximum opportunities to learn in different ways. Students benefit from exposure to modes of learning that differ from their own: The student whose intelligence is clearly interpersonal will do well in a cooperative group, but should also learn how to focus on a written report. The following are the major considerations for choosing a strategy:

- *Efficiency:* Is this the best way to ensure that the students learn the skills and knowledge to the maximum depth in the time available?

Exploit your repertoire of instructional strategies and adapt them fluidly to the kind of knowledge and skills you want to develop in the students.

- *Faithfulness to the subject matter:* Is this the best way for the students to learn this particular topic?

- *Opportunities for learning:* Have I varied my strategies so that the visual, aural, and kinesthetic learners (as well as all the others) understand the topic and have acquired the skills?

The following are notes on the qualities of different teaching strategies. It is not an exhaustive list of strategies nor of their advantages and disadvantages. The list just gives you a sense of the richness of the teaching repertoire available to you.

*Lecture* works for imparting information that all group members need and that is not otherwise available without a great deal of individual effort. The much-maligned lecture could and should be used when a lot of people need the same information. It is amusing to hear workshop leaders apologize for lecturing teachers, saying that they are not practicing what they preach—usually cooperative, hands-on, discovery learning. But they are using the lecture method because it is the most efficient in the circumstances—giving all the workshop participants the same information and thus saving everyone's time.

The lecture method got a bad name because it was the *only* teaching strategy we knew. We should use it sparingly and make sure any "lecture" uses plenty of visuals, but it shouldn't lose its place in the repertoire of teaching skills.

Lecture also gives you an opportunity to teach students how to listen attentively and take notes. It's best used only for a short time, *never more than 15 minutes.* Research has established that humans absorb information only for about a quarter of an hour, and then there's a drop-off. No, you can't lengthen that span—you've got to vary the activity.

*Cooperative learning in groups* is suited to situations where two, three, or four heads are better than one. Students should have a question to answer that can be divided into sections so that each can tackle part of it; they should have clear roles, expectations, and timetables; and they should know how to work together. If they don't know how to cooperate, then that training must be incorporated into the group's activities. Students don't automatically fall into cooperation—it's a skill we all have to learn, and there are excellent techniques for teaching it.

Don't be dismayed by the occasional student who simply won't work in a group, for whatever reason. Assign the student a research question that will occupy the same amount of time as that given to the groups. The student may see that she can't learn as much as the group members do in the same time, or she may be so inner-directed that she never notices. In any case, don't force any student to join a group.

*Discovery learning* should be used when the process of discovery genuinely helps students to learn. Conducting scientific experiments is the classic case of seeing for yourself. But it's pointless for students to "discover" well-known historical or geographic facts. And even in science, some major ideas such as evolution don't lend themselves to discovery—unless you've got a few million years to spend learning it.

*Hands-on learning,* like discovery learning, should be used carefully and not regarded as the be-all and end-all of teaching techniques. It is true that babies learn hands-on, and that manipulatives are essential for the early (and sometimes the late!) learning of mathematics, but hands-on can become an activity for the activity's sake rather than as part of learning. Here are some questions to ask yourself when planning a hands-on session:

> What *exactly* do I expect students to learn from this?
>
> Have I structured the activity so that they will learn what is intended?
>
> Are there other ways of teaching what the students should learn, and are any of them more efficient than this activity?

*Skill-and-drill workbook* learning should be used only when a particular skill is needed for the answering of a question. For example, students might need to know how to calculate cubic measures and what the concept means in order to perform a task. You would of course find out whether they do understand and can calculate cubic measures before you begin. If some don't, they may need a little solitary workbook drill just to get them familiar enough with the algorithm for calculating cubic measures. *Note, however, that skills should be taught in the context of need: Don't start with the algorithm for cubic measures and then apply the skill. First show why it's needed, and then provide the way to acquire the skill.*

*Socratic or Paideia seminars* teach discussion techniques; respect for others' opinions; close attention to a text; and oral skills. But they are time-consuming and without tight leadership can wander around the topic . In this unit, you might think about a Socratic seminar on a central document, such as the understanding of property rights as grounded in the U.S. Constitution, because all the students need to understand it thoroughly. Make sure that every student says something in the course of the seminar.

*Etc.* The many other pedagogical techniques at any teacher's command can be mixed and matched. These include class discussion, which needn't be as rule-bound as a Socratic seminar, but must be controlled and focused; reciprocal teaching, a strategy that teaches poor learners the successful strategies of expert learners; an emphasis on problem-solving as a major student activity ("So who are you going to interview to find out where our drinking water comes from?"); the use of lots of graphic organizers in the students' environment, such as a timeline showing the historical development of the idea of a public water supply; and community-based instruction, which isn't just the usual field trip, but a structured opportunity for students to learn from people on the job—perhaps, in this case, a chance to spend half a day monitoring the quality of the county's water.

All these pedagogical techniques could be enhanced by *technology,* which means not only computers with all the software you can think of (Hypercard, graphics, electronic portfolios, and so on), but also videodisk, satellite hook-ups and distance learning.

The choice of strategies is your call. It depends. (See the next section for more of this irritating phrase!) Teachers know their students and know how

> Vary your teaching so that all the students reach the standards. They won't get there in the same way or at the same time, but they must get there.

> Beware. We educators are programmed to "cover the book." Don't. It doesn't work.

they learn. *Use your judgment to vary your teaching so that all the students reach the standards. They won't get there in the same way or at the same time, but they must get there.*

This may be a new idea for you, but it is the force behind standards-driven instruction. The system is no longer intended to select and sort students so that some become laborers and others college professors, but to enable them *All* to reach the standards. (Then they can decide what they want to do at least for their first occupation—our students will have at least seven jobs in their long lifetimes.) They will *all* need the skills and knowledge embodied in the standards to live successfully in the twenty-first century. Your flexibility in switching from strategy to strategy as you see learning happening (or not happening) is going to be a major factor in your students' success.

## How Long Should the Unit Be?

A unit is as long or as short as you think necessary to complete the task. If you've mapped out your outcomes for the entire year, you will be able to estimate how much time you need to give to a single unit. Some units are a week long, some seven weeks long, some a whole semester. But it won't always be the same.

You may get a bit frustrated because so much is up to you. The length of the unit, the kinds of instruction, the way you split up your students, and even the modes of assessment are going to be your choice. The answer to "How long should this unit be?" is the same as for all the other questions of this kind: "It depends." It depends on how long it takes your students to reach the standards. It depends on the level of their previous knowledge and skills. It depends on the task, where the task fits with the other units during the year, where the students are intellectually, and the wide range of techniques—from computer-assisted instruction to cooperative learning—you must use for all students to learn.

Beware. We educators are programmed to "cover the book." DON'T. It doesn't work. It takes a long time to learn in depth, often much longer than we have planned, and we tend to get nervous and rush. You will estimate the length of your unit, but actually you will assess your students to see what they are learning and adapt your instruction, and therefore your time, according to your students' needs. Less is more...and less takes longer.

## How Does Flexible Scheduling Work?

Instruction has historically taken place in regularly spaced, predictable, totally inflexible bits of time: periods. All periods were basically of equal time, with some classes lasting perhaps two periods. Student schedules were fixed for the year, and students followed those same schedules day after day. Instruction and learning was at the mercy of those time bits, with teachers and students adapting their work so that it could be stuffed into the set period. That's a difficult way to do business! Time should—and can—be designed to fit the needs of the learner, the instruction, the experience of learning. Teachers need to be able to use instructional time flexibly, and there are many different ways to do that.

The more uninterrupted time that teachers control, the greater the options for flexible use of time. Uninterrupted time means portions of the day in which students and teachers stay put for extended periods of time with no movement in and out of that group. Every time a teacher or student moves in and out of the group at a fixed time, the opportunities for flexible scheduling on a full continuum are somewhat restricted. With lots of movement in and out of the block of time, you will have increasing time restrictions. Try to get large blocks of time for the full group of students and all teachers involved in the unit.

But you can make instruction work with a less radical approach. The simplest adaptation is *block scheduling,* with two teachers sharing two classes of students for two periods. For example, Teacher A's first period class is scheduled into Teacher B's second period class. And Teacher B's first period class is scheduled into Teacher A's second period class. This can be done quite easily within a traditional schedule, and by coordinating scheduling and grouping the two teachers can then vary time within those two periods and can group and regroup students, within their two classes, according to what is most appropriate for instruction.

> The more uninterrupted time that teachers control, the greater the options for flexible use of time.

## What About Flexible Grouping?

Flexible time frames, controlled by two or more teachers, have an added gift: the opportunity for flexible student grouping based on what is best for learning, not because a computer assigned them to a group for a year. By coordinating efforts, teachers can facilitate instruction in large groups or cozy little groups. They can provide personalized schedules that allow individuals to move through the day in their own time frame and can freely flow students between a variety of heterogeneous groups and groups that are leveled for more tightly focused instruction based on similar need.

You do this by developing various types of groups and then moving those groups to particular places for designated time periods. You *do not* have to develop individual schedules for all students! Here are the basics of group schedules:

> By coordinating efforts, teachers can facilitate instruction in large groups or cozy little groups.

- Divide students into groups, naming or numbering each group.

- Post lists of students so they will know what group they are in.

- Post a schedule that tells each group the location, teacher, and times they should arrive and leave.

If you want a different grouping of students or perhaps a different number of groups, simply design and post a different list (such as snakes, cats, horses, dogs, and mice—kids love coming up with interesting names for groups). The groups can vary in size, and there is no limit to the ways you can assign students.

The theory is simple: Design groups of students and move those groups, telling both students and teachers where to go, which teacher will facilitate, when to arrive, and when to leave.

In short, find ways to design time and grouping as a tool to enhance learning.

## What About Resources and Materials?

One thing will now have become completely clear to you: This isn't textbook, read-the-chapter-and-answer-the-questions-at-the-end learning. In fact, textbooks have lost their premier status and become only one among many resources for learning.

Standards-driven learning is intended to break down the barriers between the classroom and students' lives, so that what they learn in school explains and enhances what they experience outside. This will probably be more difficult for students to understand than for teachers, because students are so used to artificial "school" behaviors that they will resist schooling that is not boring and irrelevant!

But breaking down those barriers will be fun for you as the teacher. For standards-driven learning, newspapers, the TV news, your friends' and colleagues' concerns become the material for teaching. One of our colleagues is making a project of searching the Sunday newspapers for "triggers" and showing how they can translate into culminating tasks.

This doesn't mean that traditional resources such as the library will be neglected. To the contrary, they will get used more as students search for answers to questions meaningful to them. But libraries will be supplemented by resources both in and outside the community. Here are some ideas:

*Standards-driven learning is intended to break down the barriers between the classroom and students' lives, so that what they learn in school explains and enhances what they experience outside.*

### Databases Available on Computers

Students—and you as the teacher—have whole world of resources at your fingertips through databases. Entire encyclopedias, dictionaries, and library catalogs are available. Purchase the necessary software, make sure you know how to use a modem, and go to it.

### Communication by E-Mail

Students can talk to experts and to other students through modems and e-mail. While these connections are frequently used to enhance students' understanding of other groups (e.g., Alaskan natives or Russians), they are also sources of information and therefore important resources for learning. Some e-mail systems such as America OnLine (AOL) permit access to a large number of people, so that you could "broadcast" a question and thus find experts you didn't know existed.

### Community Resources

Every town has a history and someone who keeps it. The local librarian usually knows who this is and where all the information is kept. Students should also know how to use official community records, such as those recording sales and ownership of land; births, marriages, and deaths; and records of unusual events such as fires, floods, or diseases that affected the community. The library will have files of the local newspaper, possibly even old publications that are now defunct.

### Oral History and Local Heroes

Students should find out who knows about the town's informal history and should learn how to use the appropriate technology to record what these (frequently old) people have to say. As we know, one group of students in Georgia found fame and fortune by recording the history and folklore of their community in the *Foxfire* anthologies. Every community, every family has someone who can provide for students the background they need to understand why things are the way they are now. Students will find these people if they are encouraged and given leads.

### Business and Industry

Since business people and captains of industry have become interested in schools, they can help with more than money. They can be asked to explain the mathematics of accounting and actuarial calculations; the science behind a manufacturing process; the history of that manufacturing process and why it takes its present form; how to manage risk; the laws affecting business, farming, or industry; and the international connections essential to success, among many other matters. If business people, farmers, or industrial managers explain these things, students may perceive an answer to the age-old question, "Why do I have to learn this stuff? I'm never going to use it!"

### Local Colleges and Universities

An important part of present educational reform is making a single K–16 system out of two not-speaking systems, K–12 and post-secondary. While contacts are going on at high administrative levels, teachers and students can contribute to the continuity of the system by using the professors, libraries, laboratories, and other resources at local colleges and universities as much as possible. Teachers tend to think only of the education departments of higher education because they were nurtured there, but it's the college of letters and science that is going to be the best resource for students. Get them into the habit of telephoning a professor with a specific question, or asking if they can visit a laboratory or studio.

### Newspapers, Newsmagazines, TV News

Do you know that less than 25 percent of the population now reads a newspaper regularly? Yet newspapers are mines of information about much more than daily occurrences. They have regular sections on developments in science and even mathematics: *The New York Times* had a thoroughly understandable explanation of a famous mathematical puzzle, Fermat's last theorem, in July 1993 when a British professor produced a proof.

As we mentioned above, one of our colleagues is looking at the local Sunday newspapers to find triggers for tasks. The local newspaper is especially valuable for information about the local manifestations of global problems, such as pollution, acid rain, and economic recession.

### The Students Themselves

And finally, don't forget the students themselves as resources. Students have all kinds of interests that they sometimes don't mention to their teachers because of that barrier we mentioned above—the one keeping school apart from the real world. A student who knows baseball statistics is a great resource for mathematics, but may not know it. Students may have immense knowledge about pop music and not realize that it can be analyzed in these

> And finally, don't forget the students themselves as resources.

ways: musically; for the meaning of the lyrics; and as a reflection of changes in society. They may know a great deal about heroes and heroines we have never heard of or never considered heroic.

And what they care about can become the heart of a learning task. It probably won't be in the form the student would use to express it, but the kernel of the idea will be there: power and responsibility between parents and children, for example; or free will and determinism in the development of character.

Resources and materials are everywhere, once you begin to look. Of course there are plenty in the school—the textbooks, computers, videotapes, films that can be looked at in a new way, as triggers or as suggestions. Above all, in the school there are people, teachers, principals, janitors, parents, students, who each have something to contribute to students' learning.

### *Look at an Example of Completed Learning Section*

Let's just look at one example of a learning section, taken from "This Land Is Your Land, This Land Is My Land!"

## Learning Section One: Public Opinion Poll

### *The Task for Public Opinion Poll*

Develop an instrument and process for measuring public opinion concerning the local community's understanding of the issues regarding individual use of chemicals and the purity of water supply and their practices. What does the community know, what do they think, and what do they actually do? Collect and interpret data, including use of charts and graphs for clarity, so that the public can understand clearly what you find.

Teachers: Math, Social Studies, Language Arts, Technology

Timing: This can occur at the same time as Learning Section Two on the water cycle.

### *Standards and Components for Public Opinion Poll*

**Mathematics**

- Students understand and accurately use statistics.

  - *systematically collect, organize, and describe data*
  - *construct, read, and interpret tables, charts, and graphs*
  - *make inferences and convincing arguments that are based on data analysis*
  - *evaluate arguments based on data analysis*
  - *develop an appreciation for statistical methods as powerful means for decision making.*

**Language Arts**

- Students read a wide variety of material, including technical information needed to complete projects.

  - *know jargon and specialized language used in mathematics, social studies, science, and technology*

- Students speak and write to communicate information and ideas to various audiences for various purposes.
  - *write and speak to persuade*
  - *write and speak to inform*

**Workplace Skills**

- Students can find and use the information they need to meet specific demands, explore interests, or solve specific problems.

**Social Studies**

- Students observe, analyze, and interpret human behaviors to acquire a better understanding of self, others, and human relationships.

### Instructions for Public Opinion Poll

| Activities | Instruction |
|---|---|
| • Introduction to use of statistics | • Introduction to power of statistics in real world by rotating through centers, demonstrating actual uses of statistics followed by question-answer session<br>• Pretest students to determine current skills<br>• Analyze gaps and teach to specific areas of weakness using textbooks, computers, video instruction, and other; include extended school classes for students who need extra time to learn; pay attention to matching learning styles and teaching styles<br>• Assess by portfolio task and on-demand prompts |
| • Research current trends and issues to collect information as basis for formulating questions to use in opinion poll | • Introduction to using technology for research, taught by student technology experts<br>• Use sources for gathering data both in school and in libraries throughout community<br>• Use Internet to gather data, using cooperative learning work groups that are heterogeneous, with student tech experts in each group<br>• Interview local experts and on AOL using on-line conferencing<br>• Collectively organize research into key issues and topics by setting up mini reference library for all students to use throughout project, using vertical file and computer |
| • Use public opinion poll to collect data on public knowledge, opinions, and practices, using appropriate sampling process | • Study sampling and make selection of most appropriate method for this project<br>• Study methods of collecting data (i.e., mailing, telephone, interview, etc.) and select best method or methods for collecting data, based on hands-on experience<br>• Learn to collect additional information and disaggregate data according to various information, such as gender, age, political party, etc.<br>• Develop and implement final plan for sampling population and collecting data |

## Instructions for Public Opinion Poll (continued)

- Organize and interpret data

  - Pretest skills on using database and spreadsheet programs, use to make assignments to workgroups so all skill areas are accessible within each group; instruction in heterogeneous groups, using extended time if necessary
  - Students set up organization system for managing large amounts of data, including a personnel structure for work and file system for data
  - Use cooperative learning groups to accomplish work, with all students responsible for demonstrating proficiency in technology and in use of statistics
  - Students learn to construct charts and graphs from spreadsheet, with direct instruction, including hands-on computer centers
  - Groups present draft results using graphs and charts, making corrections based on feedback from whole group; individualized remedial instruction is identified based presentations
  - Students combine all data and prepare charts, graphs, and interpretation as individual exam; students make corrections and agree on a single report of final results

- Write analysis and conclusions, including charts and graphs to support those conclusions

  - Visiting professor lecture on making conclusions based on data
  - Socratic seminar to discuss possible interpretation of data
  - Write individual paper of conclusions based on combined data, with the focus on using data to target existing practices, areas where the public lacks information, or opinions that might be addressed in their proposal for action to be presented on Pure Water Day

- Develop presentation for public

  - Workgroups plan presentation format
  - Draft presentations presented to focus groups, with responses used to alter presentation
  - Finalize presentations and dump to video format

## The Rubric for Public Opinion Poll

*Highest score*

The results show a convincing command of the systematic collection, organization, and description of data. There is a complete understanding of the issues involved in ways to gather information about human behavior. The student has understood what information was needed and also how to craft questions to get at it. The display of data is entirely appropriate and completely persuasive.

*Next-to-highest score*

The work shows a competent command of the systematic collection, organization, and description of data. Most of the issues involved are understood. The student's ability to find information, to craft questions and convey results is clear, but may not inspire admiration.

*Next-to-lowest score*

The work shows patchy, inconsistent understanding of the systematic collection, organization, and description of data. Some of the issues are understood, but some of the questions are less focused than others. The student's ability to find information and convey results is sometimes clear, but not always.

*Lowest score*

The work shows little or no understanding of the systematic collection, organization, and description of data. One or two of the issues are understood, but barely, and the questions are unfocused. There is little evidence of the student's ability to understand and use data.

First read down the activities column: It is a progression from finding out what students know about data collection and the ways of displaying data, through activities that enable them to use data collection techniques to communicate the data they have collected.

Then read the instruction column, where you will see the kinds of instructional strategies used so that students learn each of the steps listed under activities.

Please note the variety of instructional strategies and resources used: computers, mathematics textbooks, cooperative learning groups, parent volunteers, and microcomputer software.

You will find some answers to your questions about how students learn at their own speed in a heterogeneously grouped classroom. The first activity is not timed, but students are allowed to rotate through work stations to show what they know or don't know about spreadsheets, charts, and graphs. When the major instruction on data collection and display is given, all the students hear the same information in a large lecture format, but then students who need more instruction can watch a videotape of the lecture; those who want extra help can receive it in small groups after school.

When the students have prepared their plans for collecting data, they present them to their peers for discussion, so that students not only help each other, but don't feel that this is a competition where important information must be kept from others.

The collection of the raw data about what happens to substances in the soil is facilitated by transportation and by parents. Finally, as the students process the data they have collected, they go along at their own individual speed, with help where needed.

The student's progress is continually monitored and the teacher gives the student feedback on how much has been learned and how much more needs to be done. Get the students focused on the standards and help them to assess themselves: Have I collected all the data I need to make this argument? What else would I need to do? And so on.

Do you realize that, in this section, teachers have taught in the traditional teaching position (in front of their classes, in front of a blackboard, chalk in hand) a small proportion of the time? In the rest of the section, the teacher is a coach on the side: a traffic organizer to get students to the machines they need, or the after-school coaching they have requested, or to the right car for a ride to the county offices. A helpful listener as students present their plans. Quite a different role, isn't it?

## Think About the Order of Learning

Let's keep one idea clear in our minds:

*We are not cutting up our teaching segments into skills first, ideas after sequences*

Be careful. The model of schooling from which we are trying to escape was based on the assembly line in factories, a flawed model that broke down each learning task into tiny bits, the skills that are practiced in workbooks. The idea was that if students learned each little skill in sequence, ultimately they would be able to deal with ideas. It didn't work then. And it won't work now. It was a false model of learning.

The mind continuously constructs meaning. And learning is a continuous process of assimilating new knowledge and new skills into a *meaningful* schema in the learner's mind. Students don't assemble unrelated bits of information or separate skills into a sensible whole.

Skills are best taught and learned in the context of a realistic task that the student is motivated to complete. For example, if students know that they must take a position on water purity—particularly if the task has been chosen largely because the students themselves have expressed an interest in it—then learning the technique of using scientific method to select the projects with greatest potential to make change, using the mathematics needed to measure public behavior that needs to be changed, and the writing skills necessary to communicate their position will have meaning for them. They learn because they *need* the skill in order to do their work.

**Skills are best taught and learned in the context of a realistic task.**

You shouldn't worry too much, then, about sequencing from skills to ideas. The students are most likely to take a position from the beginning and modify it as they learn more and more about the topic. And they are likely to be eager to acquire the skills they need as they complete real work for a public audience.

One of teachers who helped with this manual had two boys in her class who did not know their multiplication tables. They found they couldn't operate on a task without multiplication at their fingertips. They learned the tables in a week!

## Finalize Your Unit

You are now ready to complete your unit by finalizing plans for each learning section. You are back in familiar territory here, but we encourage you to use your full bag of tricks, not just those with which you feel most comfortable. Be open to new possibilities, and focus on students achieving standards any way they possibly can.

We hope we have answered many of your questions, and given you the incentive to try new ways. The thing you must remember, however, is that you must be a risk-taker, you must develop some tolerance for ambiguity as you jump in and give this process a try, and you must create for yourself a climate in which it is acceptable to make mistakes. You will learn best by doing—just like kids do. This process is not magic, and it is not perfect. But it is a good start. Jump in and swim! The water's fine!

## Your Turn! Step Eight

1. Select one learning section, and summarize the task for that section, decide what activities students will complete in order to achieve the goal of that section, what instruction is necessary to support each activity, how time and grouping will be altered, and which teachers will work together on this section. Complete a separate chart, found in the appendix, for each learning section.

2. Continue until each learning section is complete. This is a good opportunity for teachers to be open with each other, to discuss the best ways for students to achieve standards, to learn from one another. This is where the action is!

> The thing you must remember, however, is that you must be a risk-taker, you must develop some tolerance for ambiguity as you jump in and give this process a try, and you must create for yourself a climate in which it is acceptable to make mistakes.

---

**REMINDERS**

- Focus on the learning section you feel most comfortable with first.

- Stay focused on the standards—it's easy to be distracted and to create activities that do not move students toward performing standards.

- Work cooperatively and help each other stay focused.

# Seeing the Whole

*Every year at Christmas my grandmother bought a brand new two-thousand-piece jigsaw puzzle. Everyone—moms, dads, aunts, uncles, cousins, brothers, sisters, in-laws, and grandparents—stayed up late catching up on the year's news, nibbling on goodies, and taking turns working on this year's puzzle.*

*In the middle of the living room was the card table and jigsaw puzzle with all its interlocking pieces. Pieces that started the holiday as a jumble, two thousand (unless the baby ate some) bits of colored cardboard. Pieces that slowly disappeared as they melted into a brightly colored picture that would be framed and hung in the kitchen. The pieces were gone, and only the picture was left.*

*You have before you a puzzle. Two thousand pieces in the beginning. A seamless picture in the end.*

**What You Will Learn In Step Nine**

1.  "This Land Is Your Land, This Land Is My Land!" The final copy: "This Land Is Your Land, This Land Is My Land!" includes a culminating task, standards, and learning sections.

2.  Learn to evaluate the unit. Think about what makes a good unit and learn how to assess your own unit.

---

# THIS LAND IS YOUR LAND, THIS LAND IS MY LAND!

**The Completed Unit**

1. The Culminating Task

2. The Standards

3. The Overview of Learning Sections

4. Learning Section One: The Public Opinion Poll

5. Learning Section Two: The Water Cycle

6. Learning Section Three: Scientific Inquiry

7. Learning Section Four: Persuasive Editorial

8. Learning Section Five: Planning Pure Water Day

9. Learning Section Six: Pure Water Proposal

# THE CULMINATING TASK

*Students will plan, organize, and carry out for the community a Pure Water Day. The day's activities will focus on issues of water purity in the community. These activities will be designed to answer the driving question: Is the quality of our community's water affected by individual uses of land?*

As private citizens, we use a wide variety of chemicals in and around our homes, chemicals that have the potential to pollute the earth's water supplies. We use lawn fertilizer, pesticides, household chemicals, paint, thinner, motor oil, antifreeze, and many other common chemicals. We make frequent choices about how to use these chemicals, and we make choices about how to dispose of old or excess chemicals when we no longer need them. As individuals, our choices seem insignificant. Collectively, however, we may have a major impact—either positive or negative—on the community's water supply.

Your community is struggling with finding a balance between protecting personal freedom and protecting the water supply for the good of the entire community. How can a community protect its water supply from contamination by common chemicals (such as pesticides, fertilizer, paint, paint thinner, motor oil) while maintaining individual citizens' rights to choose how they will use these chemicals in and around their homes and farms?

Your school has been asked to plan and implement Pure Water Day in order to present information and propose action about water purity in the community. As a result of your research and your proposals, you may persuade the community that water purity is in danger and regulations should be contemplated; or that the common water source is safe and no action is necessary; or that action may be needed in the future if present trends continue.

On Pure Water Day, you will design and present an informational exhibit for the public, including

1.  Models to show how water can become polluted by human activity through the water cycle.
2.  An analysis of your community's opinions and practices in relation to pure water supply and use of chemicals, including charts and graphs to interpret data.
3.  The results of scientific inquiry testing your hypothesis on proposed projects that will impact social attitudes and practices, based on information gathered in the public opinion poll.
4.  A collection of editorials, published in newspaper format, presenting student opinions on the role of law and the U.S. Constitution in balancing personal freedom vs. community welfare, specifically related to water issues.
5.  A presentation of your conclusions and your recommendations to the community for action. The project might be focused on ensuring the purity of water now or in the future, such as setting up collection points for discarded chemicals, paint, and motor oil; researching alternatives to chemical pesticides and fertilizers; or writing a children's book on the sources of water. Or your project might be focused on informing the public that there is not a problem. You should make your decision based on all the information you have collected.

## Unit Broken Into Learning Sections

**Pure Water Day: A Community Exhibition**
(Math/Science/Language Arts/Social Studies/Art/Technology)

Present informational exhibition for the public, including models of water cycle, analysis of public opinion and practices, and results of scientific inquiry exploring proposed projects that will impact social attitudes and practices, and proposals for action that will inform the community that there is not a problem or that will prevent or correct a problem now or in the future.

↑                                              ↑

**Learning Section 5**
(All teachers)
Plan for implementation of Pure Water Day.

**Learning Section 6**
(All teachers)
Prepare for project based on information you have collected and present on Pure Water Day.

↑                                              ↑

**Learning Section 3**
Inquiry
(Math/science)
Use scientific inquiry to form and test hypothesis on proposal for projects that will impact social attitudes and practices identified in public opinion poll.

**Learning Section 4**
Scientific Student Editorials
(Language Arts/Social Studies)
Present opinions on the role of law and the U.S. Constitution in balancing personal freedom vs. community welfare, specifically related to water issues.

↑                                              ↑

**Learning Section 1**
Public Opinion Poll
(Math/language arts/social studies/technology)
Develop poll to measure public opinion, knowledge, and practices. Collect and interpret data, presenting conclusions with charts and graphs.

**Learning Section 2**
Water Cycle Models
(Science/Art)
Learn about water cycle and how it gets polluted using models.

**The Standards**

## THIS LAND IS YOUR LAND, THIS LAND IS MY LAND!

### Language Arts

- Students read a wide variety of material, including technical information needed to complete projects.

  - *know jargon and specialized language used in mathematics, social studies, science, and technology*

- Students speak and write to communicate information and ideas to various audiences for various purposes.

  - *write and speak to persuade*
  - *write and speak to inform*

### Social Studies

- Students understand the democratic principles of justice, equality, responsibility, and freedom and apply them in real-life, everyday situations.

  - *understand the U.S. Constitution and its relation to law*
  - *understand major controversies in issues of individual freedom vs. needs of society*
  - *analyze and demonstrate the rights and responsibilities of a citizen in relation to society*

- Students observe, analyze, and interpret human behaviors to acquire a better understanding of self, others, and human relationships.

### Mathematics

- Students understand and accurately use statistics.

  - *Systematically collect, organize, and describe data*
  - *Construct, read, and interpret tables, charts, and graphs*
  - *Make inferences and convincing arguments that are based on data analysis*
  - *Evaluate arguments based on data*
  - *Develop an appreciation for statistical methods as powerful means for decision making*

### Science

- Students know and understand scientific methods and use them to solve real-life, everyday problems.

  - *use scientific research cycle: formulate hypothesis, design research, collect data, organize and interpret data, form conclusions based on data*
  - *use scientific inquiry to research social behaviors*

- Students complete tasks and create products that identify systems and components and the ways the parts work together.
  - *understand water cycle*
  - *understand interaction between water cycle and pollutants on earth's surface*
  - *know basic facts about the toxicity of certain chemical compounds*

**Workplace Skills**

- Students organize and plan for a purpose.
  - *distribute tasks appropriately*
  - *allocate time and prepare schedules*

- Students work with others.
  - *cooperate in small and large groups on a project*
  - *negotiate agreement where there are differences in approach*

- Students can find and use the information they need to meet specific demands, explore interests, or solve problems.
  - *collect information about facilities, etc.*
  - *research using all available methods, including technology*

- Students use computers and other kinds of technology to collect, organize, and communicate information and ideas.
  - *use databases and spreadsheets to organize raw data*
  - *use charts and graphs to interpret data*
  - *use technology to gather information*

**The Arts**

- Students use knowledge of the principles of design to communicate ideas clearly.

## Learning Section One: Public Opinion Poll

### *The Task for Public Opinion Poll*

Develop an instrument and process for measuring public opinion concerning the local community's understanding of the issues regarding individual use of chemicals and the purity of water supply and their practices. What does the community know, what do they think, and what do they actually do? Collect and interpret data, including use of charts and graphs for clarity, so that the public can understand clearly what you find.

Teachers:    Math, Social Studies, Language Arts, Technology
Timing:      This can occur at the same time as Learning Section Two on the water cycle.

### *Standards and Components for Learning Section One*
**Mathematics**

- Students understand and accurately use statistics.
  - *systematically collect, organize, and describe data*

      – *construct, read, and interpret tables, charts, and graphs*
      – *make inferences and convincing arguments that are based on data analysis*
      – *evaluate arguments based on data analysis*
      – *develop an appreciation for statistical methods as powerful means for decision making*

**Language Arts**

- Students read a wide variety of material, including technical information needed to complete projects.

      – *know jargon and specialized language used in mathematics, social studies, science, and technology*

- Students speak and write to communicate information and ideas to various audiences for various purposes.

      – *write and speak to persuade*
      – *write and speak to inform*

**Workplace Skills**

- Students can find and use the information they need to meet specific demands, explore interests, or solve specific problems.

**Social Studies**

- Students observe, analyze, and interpret human behaviors to acquire a better understanding of self, others, and human relationships.

### Instructions for Public Opinion Poll

| Activities | Instructions |
|---|---|
| • Introduction to use of statistics | • Introduction to power of statistics in real world by rotating through centers, demonstrating actual uses of statistics followed by question-answer session<br>• Pretest students to determine current skills<br>• Analyze gaps and teach to specific areas of weakness using textbooks, computers, video instruction, and other; include extended school classes for students who need extra time to learn; pay attention to matching learning styles and teaching styles<br>• Assess by portfolio task and on-demand prompts |
| • Research current trends and issues to collect information as basis for formulating questions to use in opinion poll | • Introduction to using technology for reserch, taught by student technology experts<br>• Use sources for gathering data both in school and in libraries throughout community<br>• Use Internet to gather data, using cooperative learning work groups that are heterogeneous, with student tech experts in each group<br>• Interview local experts and on AOL using on-line conferencing |

|  |  |
|---|---|
|  | • Collectively organize research into key issues and topics by setting up mini reference library for all students to use throughout project, using vertical file and computer |
| • Use public opinion poll to collect data on public knowledge, opinions, and practices, using appropriate sampling | • Study sampling and make selection of most appropriate method for this project<br>• Study methods of collecting data (i.e., mailing, telephone, interview, etc.) and select best method or methods for collecting data, based on hands-on experience<br>• Learn to collect additional information and disaggregate data according to various information, such as gender, age, political party, etc.<br>• Develop and implement final plan for sampling population and collecting data |
| • Organize and interpret data | • Pretest skills on using database and spreadsheet programs, use to make assignments to workgroups so all skill areas are accessible within each group; instruction in heterogeneous groups, using extended time if necessary<br>• Students set up organization system for managing large amounts of data, including a personnel structure for work and file system for data<br>• Use cooperative learning groups to accomplish work, with all students responsible for demonstrating proficiency in technology and in use of statistics<br>• Students learn to construct charts and graphs from spreadsheet, with direct instruction, including hands-on computer centers<br>• Groups present draft results using graphs and charts, making corrections based on feedback from whole group; individualized remedial instruction is identified based presentations<br>• Students combine all data and prepare charts, graphs, and interpretation as individual exam; students make corrections and agree on a single report of final results |
| • Write analysis and conclusions, including charts and graphs to support those conclusions | • Visiting professor lecture on making conclusions based on data<br>• Socratic seminar to discuss possible interpretation of data<br>• Write individual paper of conclusions based on combined data, with the focus on using data to target existing practices, areas where the public lacks information, or opinions that might be addressed in their proposal for action to be presented on Pure Water Day |
| • Develop presentation for public | • Workgroups plan presentation format<br>• Draft presentations presented to focus groups, with responses used to alter presentation<br>• Finalize presentations and dump to video format |

## The Rubric for Learning Section One

*Highest score*

The results show a total understanding and accuracy of student use of collecting and organizing data and in constructing charts and graphs that reflect the data. There is complete understanding of the issues involved in ways to gather information about human behavior. The student has understood what information was needed and skillfully crafted questions to get at this information. The display of data is entirely appropriate and completely persuasive.

*Next-to-highest score*

The results show a good understanding and overall accuracy of student use of collecting and organizing data and in constructing charts and graphs that reflect the data. There is general understanding of the issues involved in ways to gather information about human behavior. The student has understood what information was needed by reading a wide variety of material and using specialized language, understanding how to craft questions to get at this information. The display of data is appropriate and persuasive.

*Next-to-lowest score*

The work shows patchy, inconsistent understanding of the systematic collection, organization, and description of data. Some of the issues are understood, with reading invomplete and technical language inconsistent inaccuracy, but some of the questions are less focused than others. The student's ability to find information and convey results is sometimes clear, but not always.

*Lowest score*

The work shows little or no understanding of the systematic collection, organization, and description of data. One or two of the issues are understood to a limited degree, and the questions are unfocused and specialized language is incorrect or not present. There is little evidence of the student's ability to understand and use data.

## Learning Section Two: The Water Cycle

### The Task for Water Cycle

How does the water cycle work? Design a model explaining how water is produced and how it gets polluted. The model must communicate clearly and accurately how the water cycle works, and exactly how water can be polluted by the use and disposal of chemicals on the earth's surface.

Teachers:    Science, Art
Timing:       Depending on scheduling arrangements in your school, Learning Sections One and Two may be going on at the same time.

### Standards and Components for Learning Section Two

**Science**

- Students complete tasks and create products that identify systems and components and the ways the parts work together.
  - *understand water cycle*
  - *understand interaction between water cycle and pollutants on earth's surface*
  - *know basic facts about the toxicity of certain chemical compounds*
- Students demonstrate understanding of the effects of human activity on the environment.

**The Arts**

- Students use knowledge of the principles of design to communicate ideas clearly.

## Instructions for Water Cycle

### Activities

- Research the complexities of the water cycle, with emphasis on the water cycle in your area

### Instructions

- Check for initial knowledge and skills about water cycle
- Select appropriate reading material to develop understanding of water cycle, based on existing understanding
- Interview panel of experts, including TV weather-forecasters, water purity government official, environmental education professor, and other experts in field
- Research local newspaper over past several decades to identify patterns related to water, floods, and draughts and to track change in understanding of behavior that might result in water pollution
- Collect illustrations of water cycle from variety of sources for use as reference
- Set up permanent reference collection for school library, with all information students have collected

- Identify and quantify possible pollutants

- Identify possible pollutants used locally in homes, yards, farms through wide variety of sources
- List possible practices that result in pollution
- Develop a reference chart that lists possible pollutants used in community, with possible practices for each pollutant that endanger the water
- Learn to access potential toxicity of chemicals

- Develop model for conveying understanding of water cycle and possible sources of pollution from household and yard chemicals

- Art teacher lectures and demonstrates basic principles of design for displaying information, followed by hands-on instruction
- Review possible media for developing model, with students deciding for themselves
- Instruction and assistance in use of medium for those who need it
- Develop plan for model, with feedback from peers and instructor for accuracy of information
- Construct final model, using parent volunteers to assist with individual coaching and special materials

## Rubric for Learning Section Two

### Highest score

The display not only shows a complete understanding of the water cycle and what can make it toxic through human activity, but also a mastery of the principles of design.

### Next-to-highest score

The work shows an understanding of the water cycle and how it can become toxic through human activity. The visual display is competent, but not inspired.

### Next-to-lowest score

The work shows some understanding of the water cycle and how it can become toxic through human activity, but the understanding is not consistent and the display may reveal incomplete understanding of the system.

### Lowest score

The work shows little or no understanding of the water cycle and how it can become toxic, and the visual display does not communicate how the system works.

## Learning Section Three: Scientific Inquiry

### *The Task for Scientific Inquiry*

Use scientific inquiry to test hypothesis about which practices need to be changed if we are to ensure pure water or what information the public is lacking or what misinformation needs to be corrected. Use the public opinion poll data to identify possible target areas in which a project might have impact and to use as a basis for formulating a hypothesis.

| | |
|---|---|
| Teachers: | Science, Math |
| Timing: | Learning Sections Three and Four can go on at the same time, depending on school schedule. Or, some students might concentrate first totally on scientific inquiry (Learning Section Three) while others concentrate totally on developing and presenting personal opinions (Learning Section Four), then reverse the groups. |

### *Standards and Components for Learning Section Three*

**Science**

- Students know and understand scientific methods and use them to solve real-life, everyday problems.

    - *use scientific research cycle: formulate hypothesis, design research, collect data, organize and interpret data, form conclusions based on data*
    - *use scientific inquiry to research social behaviors*

**Workplace Skills**

- Students can find and use the information they need to meet specific demands, explore interests, or solve problems.

    - *collect information about facilities, etc.*
    - *research using all available methods, including technology*

- Students use computers and other kinds of technology to collect, organize, and communicate information and ideas.

    - *use databases and spreadsheets to organize raw data*
    - *use charts and graphs to interpret data*
    - *use technology to gather information*

**Instructions for Scientific Inquiry**

| Activities | Instructions |
|---|---|
| • Expand understanding, skills, and sophistication in using scientific inquiry cycle | • Look at examples and nonexamples<br>• Complete performance assessment open-response task to measure knowledge of using scientific inquiry to solve real problems<br>• Group students who need further instruction in homogeneous groups to learn basic concepts, using portfolio task as method of instruction; students who understand the basics will develop materials for instruction in scientific inquiry for elementary students and implement them in elementary school<br>• Collect reference materials for use in applying scientific inquiry in this project |
| • Formulate a hypothesis about practices or information that needs to be changed | • Use conclusions from public opinion poll and understanding of water cycle and possible pollutants to identify potentially harmful practices or areas of misinformation/lack of information that needs to be corrected<br>• Study chapters in textbook on formulating and testing the hypothesis, including test<br>• Students choose to work in groups or individually on scientific inquiry and begin by learning how to formulate hypotheses<br>• Monitor student's hypothesis by peer review using scoring rubric<br>• Complete final hypothesis based on feedback |
| • Formulate plan for conducting research to test hypotheses | • Lecture on process of designing research, with seminar-style breakout sessions so students can choose what additional information they need<br>• Study similarities and differences in data to be collected for scientific inqury project and data collected for opinion poll, including how technology should be used<br>• Use scoring guide to evaluate sample research plans<br>• Develop draft plan and score according to same scoring plan before presenting final draft to instructor for design approval |

## Rubric for Learning Section Three

*Highest score*

The work shows complete understanding of scientific inquiry, including all the steps. The student has formulated a testable hypothesis, has designed a research plan, and gathered data in multiple ways to come to a reasonable conclusion.

*Next-to-highest score*

The work shows evidence of the scientific method of inquiry, but it doesn't display confidence in its use. There is a hypothesis, a research plan, but the collection of data may not be extensive or varied, and the conclusion may be obvious.

*Next-to-lowest score*

The work shows that the student knows something about the scientific method of inquiry, but is uncertain about the steps or their sequence. Pieces may be missing, and a conclusion may either be lacking or not defensible.

*Lowest score*

The work shows no understanding of the scientific method of inquiry. Data may be collected, but without a plan and without clear connection between data and conclusion.

## Learning Section Four: Persuasive Editorial

*The Task or Persuasive Editorial*

What is the appropriate balance between individual rights and community good in relation to our local water supply? Write a persuasive editorial based on a study of the U.S. Constitution and law, your research in Learning Section One, and your understanding of the water cycle and pollution is Learning Section Two. Working together, you will design, lay out, and publish the collected editorials in newspaper format for dissemination on Pure Water Day.

Teachers: Social Studies, Language Arts

*Standards and Components for Learning Section Four*

**Language Arts**

- Students speak and write to communicate information and ideas to various audiences for various purposes.

  – *write and speak to persuade*

**Social Studies**

- Students understand the democratic principles of justice, equality, responsibility, and freedom; apply them in real-life, everyday situations.

  – *understand the U.S. Constitution and its relation to law*
  – *understand major controversies in issues of individual freedom vs needs of society*
  – *analyze and demonstrate the rights and responsibilities of a citizen in relation to society*

**Workplace Skills**

- Students can find and use the information they need to meet specific demands, explore interests, or solve problems.

  - *collect information about facilities, etc.*
  - *research using all available methods, including technology*

## Instructions for Persuasive Editorial

| Activities | Instructions |
|---|---|
| • Study U.S. Constitution and Bill of Rights, focusing on the rights of the individual vs. community rights and responsibilities | • Group lecture for information<br>• Use centers to present individual reading materials, videos, filmstrips, computer programs<br>• Read historical novel dealing with issues surrounding the founding of United States<br>• Attend live theater or movie dealing with the rights of individual vs. community rights<br>• Small and large group discussions on interpretation of Constitution and meaning of conclusions |
| • Write personal opinion in persuasive style | • Read examples of good editorial articles and debate how people are best persuaded to change their opinions<br>• Compare persuasive writing in United States in last part of eighteenth century and today<br>• Whole class discusses options for writing persuasive editorials and selects writing partner or writing group<br>• Review writing process, with assessment to identify areas of weakness and seminars offered for particular writing needs<br>• Write sample paragraphs and critique, using writing portfolio scoring guide<br>• Write editorial, using brainstorming, drafting, peer review of drafts, editing in groups<br>• Final product scored, revised for technical corrections if necessary, and submitted to newspaper staff for publication |
| • Complete layout in newspaper format | • Lecture and demonstration by local newspaper, with emphasis on impact of placement in paper and layout as powerful ways to change opinion<br>• Journalism and art students coordinate and supervise completion of layout, using extended school time as necessary |

## Rubric for Learning Section Four

*Highest score*

The work shows complete knowledge of the basis of individual rights and social responsibility in the U.S. Constitution, and evidence of additional research into the issues. The statement of opinion is written so persuasively—with eloquence, supporting arguments, and clear logic—that the reader is convinced.

*Next-to-highest score*

The work shows knowledge of the basis of rights and responsibilities in the U.S. Constitution, but other research is limited. The statement of opinion shows command of persuasive writing, although without much eloquence and imagination. It is workmanlike rather than inspired.

*Next-to-lowest score*

The work shows some understanding of the basis of rights and responsibilities in the U.S. Constitution, but it is shaky, and there is no additional research. The statement of opinion does not persuade, although it does include some of the necessary components.

*Lowest score*

The student does not understand the U.S. Constitution and its relationship to law. No other research has been done, and there is no evidence that the student understands how to write persuasively.

## Learning Section Five: Planning Pure Water Day

*The Task for Planning Pure Water Day*

Develop and implement a plan for putting on Pure Water Day for the community, focusing on public awareness of the event and a high level public participation.

Teachers: All teachers

*Standards and Components for Learning Section Five*
**Workplace Skills**

- Students organize and plan for a purpose.
  - *distribute tasks appropriately*
  - *allocate time and prepare schedules*

- Students work with others.
  - *cooperate in small and large groups on a project*
  - *negotiate agreement where there are differences in approach*

- Students can find and use the information they need to meet specific demands, explore interests, or solve problems.
  - *collect information about facilities, etc.*
  - *research using all available methods, including technology*

**The Arts**

- Students use knowledge of the principles of design to communicate ideas clearly.

    *Note: Planning for Pure Water Day is a collective group activity. To get scores for individual students' contribution, teachers will need to keep observational notes and ask students to complete questionnaires on their own and on their colleagues' success in cooperating on the job.*

## Instructions for Planning Pure Water Day

| Activities | Instructions |
|---|---|
| • Students develop organizational structure | • Students learn brainstorming and problem-solving techniques<br>• Decide organizational structure and how assignments will be made<br>• Students use process to assign jobs |
| • Students plan budget | • Get preliminary budget amount and draft budget categories<br>• Develop system for budget requests<br>• Collect requests and develop final budget<br>• Review options and select site for exhibitions and for presentations |
| • Students plan physical site and equipment | • Prepare site, including equipment needs<br>• Students organize parent and community volunteers to assist<br>• Artistic design and communication strategies planned in relation to physical display<br>• Develop plan to set up on and before Pure Water Day |
| • Students engage the public | • Brainstorm options for public engagement<br>• Break into groups such as radio, newspaper, telemarketing, etc., with expert from community as resource for each group<br>• Groups plan and implement strategy, using coordinating council for coherence |

## Rubric for Learning Section Five

### Highest score

The work is planned and carried out with efficiency, economy of means, and interpersonal harmony. The letters to community members are charming and compelling, and the programs and information materials show originality and understanding of attractive communication.

### Next-to-highest score

Students organize and plan so their work is completed on time and is accomplished efficiently, although without flair. The letters and materials do their job, but no more.

### Next-to-lowest score

Students are inconsistent in their ability to organize work and allocate time to get it all completed, although the deficiencies would not cause a complete disaster. The letters are not polished, and the materials have mistakes and inaccuracies.

### Lowest score

The work is not complete, letters and materials are unsatisfactory; the presentation would be a disaster.

## Learning Section Six: Prepare Presentation of Final Proposal

### The Task for Presentation of Final Proposal

Prepare a presentation of your final proposal, to be made in a public forum on Pure Water Day. Your proposal should be based on your understanding of the water cycle and possible pollution, your research on community practices and opinions, the results of your scientific inquiry, and your position on the rights of the individual citizen in relation to the good of the community in relation to the water supply. You will present your proposal to a scoring committee on Pure Water Day, with the public welcome to attend.

| | |
|---|---|
| Teachers: | Language Arts, Social Studies, Math, Science, Art, Technology, Speech |
| Timing: | Both Learning Section Five and the preparation phase of Learning Section Six occur at the same time. |

### Standards and Components for Learning Section Six

#### Language Arts

- Students speak and write to communicate information and ideas to various audiences for various purposes.

    - *write and present orally to persuade*
    - *know and use common rhetorical forms, in this case, proposals*

**Workplace Skills**

- Students can find and use the information they need to solve problems.

  - *collect information about facilities and resources*
  - *research using all available methods*

- Students use computers and other kinds of technology to communicate information and ideas.

  - *use charts and graphs to display data*

**The Arts**

- Students use knowledge of the principles of design to communicate ideas clearly.

## Instructions for Preparation of Final Proposal

| Activities | Instructions |
|---|---|
| • Write a synopsis of proposal | • Review what students have learned in Sections One through Four, with students choosing seminars, individual review of written material, or other options based on personal learning preference<br>• Develop individual draft proposals approximately one to two pages long<br>• Critique proposals in groups, using problem-solving strategies<br>• Defend logic of proposal in student forums, varying size of group and type of forum to meet individual needs<br>• Complete final draft proposal, using writing process |
| • Develop presentation | • Select from prepared format or design personal format for presentation, with time limited to ten minutes<br>• Speech students use videotape to demonstrate basic techniques and to coach peers who request assistance<br>• Use peers, teachers, parents, comunity volunteers for rehearsal and coaching<br>• Prepare schedule for presentation |
| • Make presentation on Pure Water Day | • Present proposal for action project to community panel for scoring |

## Rubric for Learning Section Six

*Highest score*

The proposal is so persuasively argued and clearly presented that the reviewers want to implement the project. The oral presentation is polished and accompanied by visual displays, charts, and graphs, designed to make the activities and expected results clear and important.

*Next-to-highest score*

The proposal is argued clearly, but lacks persuasive power. The reviewers would not implement the project. The oral presentation has some visual displays, charts, and graphs, but their connection to the proposed activity is not completely clear.

*Lowest score*

The proposal is not argued clearly or persuasively and the reviewers would not implement the project. The oral presentation has a few visual displays, charts, and graphs, but their connection to the proposed activity is purely coincidental.

## Pure Water Day

Finally, students present Pure Water Day to the community, the culmination of all their work. They exhibit the results of the learning sections, in addition to making public presentations of their proposals for creating or maintaining pure water in their community.

\*    \*    \*

## Learn to Evaluate the Unit

You have seen the sample unit in its entirety, and you have before you a unit that you have completed. You have a culminating task that is closely aligned with the standards you have selected. And you have backward mapped that task into chunks of instruction called learning segments. You have clearly defined each learning task by planning instruction and writing a rubric for scoring the task.

You've been through all this work in order to produce a unit. Now you'll continue to produce more units, and so will you colleagues. You need a guide to make sure you have good units, units that can be taken by any teacher and used with the assurance that they will get students to standards. Here's a list of the important components in a good unit, a list you can use to evaluate your unit.

### Is the Unit Complete?

The unit presents the culminating task and the driving questions at the beginning. The standards and components are listed for the unit as a whole and for each learning section. Rubrics for all sections to be assessed are fully written out. The explanatory material places the unit within a range of suitable grades ("middle school" or "high school").

### *Do the Students Learn Standards?*

The unit naturally and clearly moves students toward successful performance on the rigorous learner standards you have selected for this unit. Students will be able to tell you exactly what they are learning, and the instruction is varied enough to meet a wide variety of learning styles and skill levels.

### *Are the Standards Naturally Integrated?*

The culminating task and all the learning sections have standards and components clearly listed, and they allow students to work in situations where different subjects are unified naturally. The task is real, not artificial, and learning is enhanced because of the integration and because of the unit. Instruction flows as a single unit rather than having fragmented, disjointed work that is connected loosely and unnaturally. The standards may be cited more than once in a unit's different learning sections.

### *Is This the Right Task?*

The unit clearly exemplifies the standards, has soundness of content, and is a measurable, real-world activity that unifies standard naturally. It provides answers to the driving questions and is interesting to students, inspiring them to learn. It links students' lives and personal concerns with larger social issues and world concerns. It may be a real problem or concern in the community where you live. The unit has purpose and audience, and students know exactly what they have to produce and who is intended to read/hear/view it.

### *Do the Learning Sections Match the Text?*

The unit is organized toward effective performance of the culminating task. All the activities necessary for the successful completion of the unit are described and matched with appropriate instructional strategies, and the learning sections identify necessary knowledge and skills. The task makes sense, and the separate pieces flow together for a single purpose. If the students were to go through the learning sections blindly, they would be able to perform the culminating task. If they could do it *without* the learning sections, you need to rethink that task! Conversely, if doing the learning sections don't lead to the task, rethink the learning sections.

### *Are Local Resources Available?*

There are local resources—universities, business people, parents you know about, local natural features such as parks, rivers, lakes, mountains, architectural monuments—that make this idea appealing for students in your area and possible for you to teach. Students learn from resources other than school and teacher, and there are both school and community reference materials and opportunities for learning. Technology is incorporated into the unit to support instruction, and opportunities for school-to-work connections are included.

### *Can You Measure Performance?*

The unit requires students to demonstrate what they have learned, and you can measure their performance on the selected standards. You can make decisions about instruction based on skill levels students perform in completing the task.

### Do the Rubrics Match the Standard?

The list of criteria in each rubric is rich enough to capture the quality of what the student is asked to do and to produce. They are not asked about completion of the task, which is assumed, nor are they be answerable with "Yes" or "No." The rubrics match the standards, even using words from the standards statements.

Now it is time to step back and learn to look at the unit as a whole, to evaluate a unit just like you evaluate student work. You will start by looking at the sample unit in its final form, and finish by evaluating your own unit.

Use the list to analyze the strengths and weaknesses of "This Land Is Your Land, This Land Is My Land!" Look for ways to improve the unit, ways you would change it to make it better. This is a perfect opportunity for discussion—probably rather heated—about how students achieve standards, how teachers can increase student achievement. Enjoy!

## Your Turn! Step Nine

1. Evaluate your unit, using the checklist (form found in Appendix B) to see if your unit meets the criteria listed as important components of a good unit.

2. Make any changes necessary to meet those criteria.

   *Note: Once you have student work from the unit, you will have to go back to Step Seven to review the process for scoring that work using your rubrics. This is an essential part of the work of the unit, but it is not a step in this process because there is not student work available at this point in your work. So, in the meantime...*

3. Celebrate! Celebrate! Celebrate!

# Appendix A

# Where to Find
# Standards Documents

## *Summary of Standards*

The Council for Basic Education has revised its popular chart entitled *Standards: A Vision for Learning* that has been distributed to more than 70,000 schools and individuals throughout the United States since 1992. The new chart lists standards in seven subjects at grades four, eight, and twelve along with a vision of what an educated person should be able to do. It is available for $2 each (volume discount) from:

Council for Basic Education (CBE)
1319 F Street NW
Washington, DC 20005
Phone: (202) 347-4171

## *National Standards*

### The Arts

The national arts education standards in dance, music, theater, and visual art, published in spring 1994, are available from:

Music Educators' National Conference
1902 Association Drive
Reston, VA 22091
Phone: (703) 860-4000
Fax: (703) 860-4826

### Civics and Government

Request standards from:

Center for Civic Education
5146 Douglas Fir Road
Calabasas, CA 91302
Phone: (818) 591-9321
Fax: (818) 591-9330

### English and Language Arts

Request standards from:

National Council of Teachers of English
111 West Kenyon Road
Urbana, IL 61801
Phone: (217) 328-3870
Fax: (217) 328-0977

### Foreign Languages

For copies of standards and other available material or information about opportunities to comment on standards, contact:

American Council on the Teaching of Foreign Languages, Inc.
6 Executive Plaza
Yonkers, NY 10701-6801
Phone: (914) 963-8830
Fax: (914) 936-1275

### Geography

Geography standards were published in October 1994 and are available from:

National Council of Geographic Education
Geography Standards Project
1600 M St. NW
Washington, DC 20036
Phone: (202) 775-7832
Fax: (202) 429-5771

### History

National standards for U.S. history are available from:

National Center for History in the Schools at UCLA
231 Moore Hall, 405 Hilgard Ave.
Los Angeles, CA 90024
Phone: (310) 825-4702

### Mathematics

The National Council of Teachers of Mathematics (NCTM) has published two volumes of standards: *Curriculum and Evaluation Standards for School Mathematics* and *Teaching Standard*. No mathematics class should be without them. Ask for a third volume, entitled *Assessment Standards for School Mathematics*. The curriculum and teaching standards and any other new publications are available from:

National Council of Teachers of Mathematics, Inc.
1906 Association Drive
Reston, VA 22091
Phone: (703) 620-9840
Fax: (703) 476-2970

**Science**

The National Committee on Science Education Standards and Assessment is developing the national science education standards, putting together the efforts of the National Science Teachers' Association and the American Association for the Advancement of Science. You may request their most recent work from:

National Academy of Sciences
National Research Council
2101 Constitution Avenue, NW  HA 486
Washington, DC 20418
Phone: (202) 334-1399

The American Association for the Advancement of Science (AAAS) has published what it calls "benchmarks" (which are standards) for Project 2061. Project 2061 is a long-term effort to improve literacy in science, mathematics, and technology. Phase 1 of the project identified the knowledge, skills, and habits of mind all students should acquire as a consequence of their school experience in grades K–12 in a book called *Science for All Americans*. You should get both *Science for All Americans* and *Benchmarks for Scientific Literacy,* in addition to any other new publication.

American Association for Advancement of Science
1333 H Street, NW
Washington, DC 20005
Phone: (202) 326-6680
Fax: (202) 371-9849

The National Science Teacher's Association is assisting in the development of science standards. For more information, contact:

National Science Teacher's Association
1840 Wilson Boulevard
Arlington, VA 22201
Phone: (703) 243-7100
Fax: (703) 243-7177

**Social Studies**

The National Council for the Social Studies is composed of elementary, secondary, and college social studies teachers. They are assisting in developing standards in social studies. For more information, contact:

National Council for the Social Studies
3501 Newark Street, NW
Washington, DC 20016
Phone: (202) 966-7840
Fax: (202) 966-2061

## *State Standards*

Kentucky has standards that are clearly stated and are used to measure school performance. These standards, called Academic Expectations, are more clearly defined by "demonstrators," plus great teaching and assessment ideas listed in *Transformations: Kentucky's Curriculum Framework*. You can also ask for current information on Academic Expectations and Content Standards. All are available from:

Kentucky Department of Education
Capitol Plaza Towers
500 Mero Street
Frankfort, KY
Phone: (502) 564-3421

California doesn't have standards or outcomes as such, but they are embedded in and drive the content of the California Curriculum Frameworks and Guidelines. For a list of them and their prices, contact:

California State Department of Education, P.O. Box 271
Sacramento, CA 95802-0271
Phone: (916) 445-1260

### District Standards

In Chicago, the Chicago Public Schools and the Chicago Teachers' Union got together with some funding from the MacArthur and Joyce Foundations and asked their teachers to come up with Learning Outcomes for Chicago students. They produced a wall chart, something like the CBE chart, which has been reviewed by school communities throughout the system. The chart is also available in a Spanish version. For copies (specify English or Spanish), contact:

Allen Bearden
Chicago Teachers' Union Quest Center
222 Merchandise Mart Plaza, Suite 400
Chicago, IL 60654-1005
Phone: (312) 329-9100

### National Organizations Related to Standards

In addition to the organizations developing national standards, there are other national organizations that can serve as a resource in helping you achieve standards-based reform. They are primary sources that can help you find out about different projects focused on improving education.

American Alliance for Health, Physical Education, Recreation and Dance
1900 Association Drive
Reston, VA 22091
Phone: (703) 476-3405
Fax: (703) 476-9527

AAHPERD is the national association for health, physical education, recreation, and dance educators.

American Association for Adult and Continuing Education
1101 Connecticut Avenue, NW Suite 700
Washington, DC 20005
Phone: (202) 429-5131
Fax: (202) 223-4579

AAACE is interested in national adult education issues.

American Association of Museums
1225 Eye Street, NW, Suite 200
Washington, DC 20005
Phone: (202) 289-1818
Fax: (202) 289-6978

AAM's services include accreditation, museum assessment programs, government affairs, continuing education, publications, and vendor-provided services.

American Council for the Arts
One East 53rd Street
New York, NY 10022-4201
Phone: (212) 223-2787
Fax: (212) 223-4415

The National Council for the Arts promotes arts and has an education division.

American Vocational Association
1401 King Street
Alexandria, VA 22314
Phone: (703) 683-3111
Fax: (703) 683-7424

The AVA is the national association for vocational education.

Association for Supervision and Curriculum Development
1250 North Pitt Street
Alexandria, VA 22314
Phone: (703) 549-9110

The ASCD provides information in the areas of curriculum, instruction, supervision, and leadership in education.

These aren't the only contacts available—just a selection so that you don't feel you're out there alone. Lots of states have standards, goals, or outcomes (sometimes all three!), and several districts as well as Chicago have standards documents. Two private groups, the Hudson Institute and the Edison Project, are also publishing standards.

These contacts will get you started. Because it is very much an evolving arena, constantly look for new information and new contacts so you will have access to the most current standards available.

# Appendix B

# Forms

Please make copies of these forms as you use them, saving the originals for future use. On each form, you have the opportunity to mark your work as "Final" or "Draft." Simply circle your choice.

**Standards and Components: Final or Draft**

Name of Unit    _____

Author(s)    _____

Standard Number  _____    Subject  _____

_____

_____

- 

- 

- 

- 

- 

Standard Number  _____    Subject  _____

_____

_____

- 

- 

- 

- 

-

**Ideas for Driving Questions**

Author(s) _____

_____

- _____

_____

- _____

_____

- _____

_____

- _____

_____

- _____

_____

**The Culminating Task: Final or Draft**

Name of Unit _____

Author(s) _____

Driving Question _____

_____

_____

Culminating Task _____

_____

_____

_____

_____

_____

_____

## Analysis of Culminating Task: Final or Draft

Name of Unit        _____

Author(s)         _____

**Do Students Learn Standards?**                      YES        NO

Does the task naturally and clearly move students toward successful performance on the rigorous learner standards you have selected for this unit? Will students be able to tell you exactly what they are learning?

**Does the Task Provide an Answer to Your Driving Question?**      YES        NO

Does the culminating task answer the driving question naturally? Does the connection make sense? Does it flow together for a single purpose?

**Does the Task Unify Standards Naturally?**               YES        NO

Does the task allow students to work in situations where different subjects are unified naturally? Is the task real or artificial? Does the instruction flow as a single unit rather than having fragmented, disjointed work that is connected loosely and unnaturally? Does the task make sense? Do the separate pieces flow together for a single purpose?

**Does the Task Motivate Students?**                   YES        NO

Would this subject interest students and make them excited about researching it? Is it interesting to most students? Is it a real problem or concern in the community where you live? Does it link students' lives and personal concerns with larger social issues and world concerns?

**Can You Measure Performance?**                     YES        NO

Will this task require students to demonstrate what they have learned? Can you measure their performance? Can you make decisions about instruction based on their level of skill in completing the task?

**Are Local Resources Available?**                    YES        NO

Are there local resources appealing to students in your area and possible for you to teach? *Where possible, students need to learn from resources other than school and teacher.* What is available that you can use? Are there school and community reference materials? Is technology available? What are the opportunities for hands-on work?

**Has Your Task a Form, Purpose, and Audience?**          YES        NO

Will students know exactly what they have to produce and who is intended to read/hear/view it? The task must result in a product that can be scored. It will be judged for its suitability for its audience as well as for the soundness of its content.

**Unit Broken into Learning Sections: Final or Draft**

Name of Unit     _____

Author(s)     _____

Learning Section Number     _____     Final or Draft     _____

Name of Unit     _____

Author(s)     _____

Task for Learning Section ____

[ ]

Standards for Learning Section ____

- 

- 

- 

- 

- 

Teacher(s) for Learning Section ____

_____

_____

Timing for Learning Section ____

_____

_____

Instruction for Learning Section _____ Final or Draft _____

Name of Unit

Author(s)

| Activities | Instruction |
|---|---|
|  |  |
|  |  |
|  |  |

Final Analysis of Unit   _____

Name of Unit:   _____

Author(s)   _____

| | | |
|---|---|---|
| 1. The Unit Is Complete | YES | NO |
| 2. Students Learn Standards | YES | NO |
| 3. Standards Are Naturally Integrated | YES | NO |
| 4. This Is the Right Task | YES | NO |
| 5. Learning Sections Match the Task | YES | NO |
| 6. Local Resources Are Available | YES | NO |
| 7. You Can Measure Performance | YES | NO |
| 8. Rubrics Match the Standards | YES | NO |

Comments

_____

_____

_____

_____

_____

_____

_____

_____

_____

# A Summary of the Nine Steps

## Step One

*Instructions:  List the learner standards for each SEPARATE subject you might possibly include in your unit. CAUTION: THIS SOUNDS SIMPLE. IT'S NOT!*

1.  You will need a package of 4 x 6 index cards and a way to color code different subjects (such as colored marker pens). A highlighter pen can also be useful.

2.  You will need copies of standards such as the *NCTM Standards,* state, district, or national standards or outcomes, textbooks, and any other materials that determine what students in your school are required to learn.

3.  List the learner standards for each subject or curriculum area that might possibly be included in your study—either for the year or for less than a year.

4.  Record every single standard on a separate card, using different colors for each subject or curriculum area. Be as concise as you can, making sure each standard is clearly stated and is fully understandable.

5.  Option: Highlight key words in standards if you choose, particularly if they are long statements.

6.  Don't lose the cards!

---

**REMINDERS**

*   Decide what your students will know and be able to do for each subject for the year or part of the year (use your textbook unit headings only if all else fails).

*   Keep your focus on standards now. Activities will follow.

*   Select only the standards for which you have time.

---

**Step Two**

*Instructions: Make sure each standard includes components that clearly define exactly what you want students to know and be able to do for each standard.*

1. List components for each standard, either expanding or simplifying eachstandard as necessary. NCTM standards are excellent examples, and California's *Curriculum Frameworks and Guidelines* and the Demonstrators in Kentucky's *Transformations* can be helpful here as examples. But any curriculum material you have that succinctly clarifies your broad standards will do the trick. (Textbooks can also serve as good examples of the process, since they have broad unit and chapter headings, with more specific subheadings in each chapter.)

2. Record each component on a separate index card and clip them to their appropriate standard cards.

3. Assign a number to each standard, and use that same number on each of the component cards that belong with that standard. Place the number in the top right hand portion of each card. This indexing will be essential when you start selecting the standards and components you will use in your unit.

---

**REMINDERS**

- List standards selected for the year's teaching.

- Decide what each standard includes.

- Outline components for each standard.

- Write in plain English.

- Write standards, not activities.

## Step Three

*Instructions: Connect learner standards (and/or components of standards) across subjects. Make connections only where working on these standards together will help students understand better than would studying them separately. Make connections both within subjects and across subjects.*

1.  Place learner standards cards in front of you, with cards from each subject in separate horizontal rows (left to right). Place each component below the appropriate standard card so that you can see all cards (sort of like playing solitaire). If you color-coded your cards, the rows will look like broad stripes on a flag! Double-check to see that all standards and matching components are given a number so you can readily connect the standards and their components.

2.  Sequence standards where necessary within each separate subject, basing your decision on essential prerequisites. Be open-minded, and sequence only what's essential. Sequence from left to right.

3.  Cluster any standards that fit together within each subject. Hint: You will have many standards that stand alone, if you have broadly stated standards. Don't expect to have everything clustered!

4.  Now try to connect standards *across* subjects for the best instructional fit. Try different combinations and discuss how instruction would make better sense to students with those combinations. Move, group, regroup, and cluster standards cards according to natural connections within and across subjects. Duplicate cards if necessary.

5.  Continue until you (or your group) have made the best connections possible for instruction. DON'T FORCE THE FIT! If the connection is not natural, let those standards remain alone.

6.  You will probably have some instances with all subjects integrated, some standards that may not be integrated, and all combinations in between. That's fine. There is no single correct way to do this!

7.  Mark your combinations of cards when you are finished (we use brightly colored removable sticker dots, in case we change our minds later) so you can remember what clusters of cards go together, clipping them together with paper clips when you store them.

8.  Your goal is to develop at least ONE good cluster of standards, a cluster that makes sense together and has potential for increasing learning, for developing a strong culminating task. One strong cluster. With experience, you will be able to identify several clusters and rough out potential units, but as a beginner you are interested only in selecting one naturally integrated cluster to use as the standards driving instruction and learning in your unit. Pick one.

---

**REMINDERS**

- Look for natural connections between subjects.

- Think of possibilities for instruction as you look for the best fit.

- Don't force the fit.

- Keep the focus on helping *all* students achieve standards.

## Step Four

*Instructions: Develop ideas for culminating tasks that can be connected to clusters of standards. Select one or more ideas, including powerful driving questions, that can be developed into a good culminating task.*

1.  Get more 4 x 6 cards and a different color of marker than you used before (or use smaller cards—you need an easy way to differentiate idea cards from standards cards). List a wide variety of ideas in the form of essential questions, projects, or problems that can be developed into culminating tasks, and write each idea on a separate card. Or cut out newspaper articles, collect video clips, select pieces of art. In short, use any source of ideas you can find.

2.  Match your clustered standards cards with ideas. Combine ideas, or write new ones. You can regroup standards as you see new possibilities.   Note: The advantage of doing the whole year at one time is that changing standards for one standards-driven unit affects the whole year.

3.  Record your different ideas for driving question(s) and draft culminating tasks using the forms included at the end of the manual.

---

### REMINDERS

- The culminating task, when completed, needs to show student mastery of the selected standards.

- Use natural connections.

- Don't worry that you didn't get it right the first time—you will learn from your mistakes.

- Collect many different ideas for tasks, and save them.

- Brainstorm! Don't reject any idea, no matter how crazy. You don't have to use it.

- Ask kids. You'll be surprised.

## Step Five

*Instructions: Fully develop the culminating task for your unit. Make sure the task perfectly matches the standards and you know all the content required by the wording of the culminating task.*

1. Select a draft culminating task. Place the task on a large table in front of you—or on the floor.

2. Place your cluster of standards on the table (or floor) so that you can see all the standards driving your unit.

3. Get several large, blank pieces of paper to do your content mapping. Start by drawing a circle in the center of the paper and writing a terse summary of your driving question/culminating task inside the circle. You might want to number the page so you can differentiate as you work through other drafts!

4. Look at the draft culminating task, and map the content. Look for all the natural possibilities within that task as it is written. Be sure to take off your rose-colored glasses and see the task as it really is! You may have made assumptions that are not written into the task.

5. Analyze the content map in relation to the selected standards. If you have a perfect fit, you can quit. Most likely, you will have to make adjustments over and over. Bounce between standards, content map, and culminating task until you have a perfectly aligned culminating task that embodies the standards. Continue to adjust the culminating task, analyze the altered task using the content map, and relate the task to standards until you have a product that is a perfect fit or until you decide to discard that draft culminating task and try another. You must have a task that embodies the standards, a task that will stand on its own when the list of standards is removed.

6. Once you have a final culminating task, fill out the Checklist for Analyzing Culminating Task at the end of the manual. Analyze the culminating task you have written using the checklist. Decide if the culminating task is complete as is, if it can be successfully adapted, or—if the match is not satisfactory—if you need to start over on the culminating task. Evaluate your culminating task according to the criteria for successful task. Make any necessary changes and finalize your culminating task accordingly.

---

**REMINDERS**

- The culminating task must totally embody the standards.

- Map the content to identify the learning potential for your idea, then shape the task to drive students learning the selected standards.

- Adjust until you have a near-perfect match.

- Use the checklist to help make improvements.

**Step Six**

*Instructions: Divide your standards-driven unit into learning sections. Base all your decisions on the culminating task, begin with the task, and move backward.*

1.  Ask yourself these questions: "What do students need to do to complete the culminating task? What do students need to do to learn the standards and components being addressed?" Look for questions that flow naturally out of the task. Use both your content map and these questions to look for the natural chunks of instruction necessary to complete the task and have students achieve standards. Get a big sheet of paper and summarize the final task, then start drawing chunks as a visual, showing the work that must flow into the final task.

2.  Once you have divided the culminating task into chunks, you have identified your learning sections. These sections might either produce a thing (like the opinion survey), knowledge of new concepts, or new ability to apply skills.

3.  Finally, decide the order in which the learning sections must occur for optimal learning. You will find that there are many choices, with some things that must be done sequentially and others where the work is somewhat independent. Give it your best shot, and you can always adjust later as you develop the instruction more specifically.

---

**REMINDERS**

- Keep standards in mind—always!

- Keep cycling back between the culminating task and the standards.

---

## Step Seven

*Instructions: Write the rubrics for your unit, developing a rubric for each separate chunk of instruction you will be scoring. Be sure the rubric matches the selected standards and the task.*

1.  Choose a scale along which you will place student work, probably a four- or six-point scale. Use an even number so there will be no midpoint.

2.  Look at the standards you want students to attain in each learning section. Use the language of the standards to design a rubric ranging from the best possible performance to the least successful performance.

3.  Decide the breaking point on the scale that indicates successful performance (or performance that requires minor assistance) and performance that demonstrates the need for reteaching.

4.  When the unit is underway, you will finalize the rubric by trying it out on some pieces of work in progress and adjusting it.

5.  After the each learning section is complete, organize a group of scorers and set aside a block of time to identify benchmark papers for each point on your scale, and then to score the students' work for that learning section.

---

### REMINDERS

*   Keep your eye on the standards as you write the rubrics.

*   Make clear to the students how their work is going to be evaluated.

*   Be prepared to explain and defend performance assessment and scoring by rubric.

*   Make it clear that you will NOT score incomplete work.

*   Show the rubric to the students as soon as you're confident with it.

## Step Eight

1.  Select one learning section, and summarize the task for that section, decide what activities students will complete in order to achieve the goal of that section, what instruction is necessary to support each activity, how time and grouping will be altered, and which teachers will work together on this section. Complete a separate chart, found in the appendix, for each learning section.

2.  Continue until each learning section is complete. This is a good opportunity for teachers to be open with each other, to discuss the best ways for students to achieve standards, to learn from one another. This is where the action is!

---

### REMINDERS

*   Focus on the learning section you feel most comfortable with first.

*   Stay focused on the standards—it's easy to be distracted and to create activities that do not move students toward performing standards.

*   Work cooperatively and help each other stay focused.

## Step Nine

1.  Evaluate your unit, using the checklist (form found in Appendix B) to see if your unit meets the criteria listed as important components of a good unit.

2.  Make any changes necessary to meet those criteria.

*Note: Once you have student work from the unit, you will have to go back to Step Seven to review the process for scoring that work using your rubrics. This is an essential part of the work of the unit, but it is not a step in this process because there is not student work available at this point in your work. So, in the meantime...*

3.  Celebrate! Celebrate! Celebrate!

# INDEX